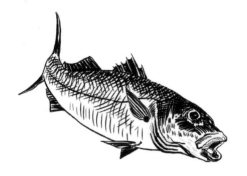

The Song of the Solitary Bass Fisher

*Ideas, tactics, and experiences
from the rocks and beaches
of a frugal all-weather Cornishman*

James 'Leakyboots' Batty

Merlin Unwin Books

Merlin Unwin Books Ltd
Palmers House
7 Corve Street
Ludlow
Shropshire SY8 1DB
UK

www.merlinunwin.co.uk

The author asserts his moral right to be identified with this work.

ISBN 978-1-910723-79-1

Typeset in 11 point Minion Pro by Merlin Unwin Books

Illustrations by Merlin Unwin

Printed by Jellyfish Print Solutions

Contents

To my wife Shelley

In spite of noises in the middle of the night, slimy clothes in the laundry basket, and the persistent hum of rotten squid in the car, she remains my best friend.

11lbs 6oz, caught in a November storm on whole squid at about 15 yards range. People who see me fishing sometimes tell me I should take casting lessons, but better bass tend to feed very close in. I'm also given tips about good rods on sale for a few hundred quid. No thanks, I do OK with my cheap tackle – the bass are in the water, they can't see what's in my hands. They can't see my lucky woolly hat either, but that's an essential bit of kit. It protects my brain, and bass fishing's a thinking game.

To catch a big cod you fling your gear miles into the surf, and that takes athleticism and coordination. For a big turbot you fork out for a charter boat and spend a few days bobbing about on the ocean wave. A big shark calls for a boat trip and some pricey kit as well. A marlin means going overseas. And that's why I love my bass: even a clumsy buffer like myself – who dislikes boats, resents expensive tackle, and hates long distance travel – can do pretty well as a bass fisher. The keys to successful bass fishing are almost all in the mind.

By the way there are a few snaps of me later in the book, but I'm not as handsome as most of my bass. Rode hard and put away wet, that's about my style.

Stay safe, and tight lines to one and all.

CHAPTER ONE

What To Expect

What's going on?

This isn't a book about how to catch bass. It's a book about how I catch bass. There's a difference.

First of all I only fish a very small patch in west Cornwall. Petrol's not cheap, I don't like driving, and I never venture more than about fifteen miles from where I live in Mount's Bay. So for all I know, what I've learned on my rocks and beaches may be useless if you fish in the *terra incognita* that lies east of the Tamar – or even east of Helston. I doubt it. It's not as if I'm baiting up with lugworm pasties or using lures that sing Trelawney, so I reckon a lot of my dodges should work almost anywhere. But I don't have the wet boots experience to back up my view; and that might be important, because some of my ideas seem to be at odds with the conventional wisdom.

I've read the classic writers – Clive Gammon, Des Brennan, John Darling, Mike Ladle – and they've given me a solid grounding of knowledge. But I'm a tinkerer, so I've used that grounding to build very personal approaches to my sport, especially in dodgy conditions. When I run into other fishers in a calm or a raging storm, they describe what I'm doing as interesting (if they're diplomatic), weird (if they're less guarded), or downright barking daft (if they're the sort of straight-talkers who call a spade a bloody shovel). I know my sometimes unusual and somewhat self-taught Cornish methods work for me. I can only hope they'll work for you too.

Second, I never fish from boats. About forty-five years ago my brother and I ran a charter-boat in East Africa, and that cured me of any possible wish to have a boat again. You don't really own a boat, it owns you. So unless you enjoy all the maintenance and trailing and suchlike, buying a boat's like starting a prison sentence. And I'm not interested in fishing from other people's boats either. A local skipper tells me his clients come back at the end of a trip and say, 'I caught a cod'; and he thinks, 'No you didn't, I caught a cod, you just reeled it in.' I'm with the skipper: finding the fish is the challenge and the fun, and I'm not going to pay a hefty charter fee to miss out on it.

Third, I don't fish live-bait very much. I hate carrying stuff, the idea of setting out like a rod-toting window-cleaner or ice-cream seller, with a big bucket or a cold-box, would be enough to keep me at home. When I come across a promising live-bait – a whiting that snaffles my worms, a sandeel scraped at the water's edge, a small mackerel or pollack that grabs my lure, a prawn or blenny in a rock-pool – I use it. But live-baiting isn't one of my staples even though I know it can be a terrific way of getting into the fish.

Fourth, as the years go by I fish more with bait than with lures or the fly. When conditions look spot-on I still take the lure-rod or the fly-rod for a wander, but my default setting's to head for a beach. I just enjoy it more. A lot of the challenges around lures and the fly are physical – mud-tromping along the coastal footpath, scrambling over slippery rocks in the dark, casting a plug into a tight spot in a gusty cross-wind, flicking a fly-line through a raging hoolie, ice-dancing on wet seaweed – which may be why younger, more athletic fishers are such fans. On the beach I do a good deal of walking – to find the fish, the better surf, the weed-free patch – but the real exercise is in the head. It's all about wondering what to try next, what the bass could be eating, where the food might be concentrating. And as I grow older I seem to prefer the mental workout.

Lastly, I'm sure I don't always fish in the most productive way, I fish in the way that makes me happiest. For instance I focus mostly on early mornings, from a couple of hours before first light. Why? Well, I catch my fair share of decent bass in that slot, and I'm pretty convinced they feed harder in the last hours of darkness than at any other time. But mostly it's because I love early mornings, when there's nobody else around, when the seals are so laid back that they sit beside me on the shore, and when I know I'll see a sunrise and a steaming hot coffee at the end of my outing.

Some folk likely will find the how-and-why stuff boring, so I've included lots of fishing stories to illustrate the way I approach my sport. They're in italics. For obvious reasons they tell of successful outings. We all have bad days, but I try not to dwell too much on the trip when I caught one tiddler and a load of weed, lost a favourite lure, half-drowned in the rain, ripped my waders on a bramble, dropped my tackle-bag in dog poo, and found my car wouldn't start. When the fishing's rotten I hope I learn something about my marks, but writing or reading about a good bass is a lot more fun.

So with all those disclaimers why am I bothering to write a book? Definitely not because I think I know everything about bass fishing. Nobody does, nobody ever will, and if they did, I'd take up snooker or competitive leek-growing instead. Bass are always going to be somewhat mysterious, that's why it's such fun to chase them. Some folk, often fishing guides, say you just need to work out 'the pattern'. Then you'll know where, when, and how to make guaranteed catches. I look at these confident assertions the same way I listen to investment bankers telling me they can predict the stock market. The pattern or the financial model is bang-on when you look at what's happened in the past. And when you look at what might happen tomorrow or next week, it's about as reliable as an election manifesto, a weight loss advertisement, or a drunken palm-reader with a fraud conviction. I don't think anyone can say with confidence what bass will do, and I'm entirely sure I can't.

No, I'm putting my ideas on paper because a lot of people have asked me to do just that. I've posted catch reports on a couple of forum sites, always with a bit of background about how I caught the fish. Then other fishers have sent me messages: 'I read what you did and I thought you were totally nuts. But I was blanking, so I decided to try some of your loopy ideas. Guess what, I had three good bass. You should write a book.' One chap suggested I collect all my posts and just bodge them together.

But that really didn't work. Quite a few of my write-ups were foul-mouthed rants about the odd half-wit surfer who manages to run over my line three times in succession on a two mile beach, or the abject dirt-bags who leave bait wrappers and balls of mono on my favourite rock marks; and most were about well-sized bass, because forum-readers always want a photo of a whopper. But a lot of my best catches have been nothing-special fish winkled out against the odds, and a lot of my best trips have been when I managed to help another fisher break a run of blanks. And I've realised that the greatest pleasure I take from my outings is when I can give someone a tip that turns defeat into victory. Best of all is when the other bod's a youngster. Grown-ups have learned to play life a bit cool (as in, 'What a pleasant surprise, I'm really quite chuffed'), but juniors wear their hearts on their sleeves (as in, 'That's totally out-effing-rageous, this is the best day of my whole life, and I'm in love with that bass.').

First light on a summer morning, I was wandering along a rough and weedy stretch in Mount's Bay, tossing a little Toby whenever I saw a swirl. The bay was jumping with whitebait, every predator in the sea had come to join the feast. I had a couple of mackerel, a pollack, and a few bass. Nothing enormous, just some good eating fish, so I kept the mackerel and a bass. Rounding an outcrop I ran into a lad of about fourteen so I stopped for a chat. He was on holiday, this was his first outing with a brand lure new outfit. He'd saved his newspaper-round money for a year to pay for it, and he'd chosen his rod, reel, braid, and lures after days of research in the on-line forums. He was fishing a big shallow-diving plug, something Japanese, expensive, and about five inches long. He'd caught two pollack and a mackerel. He looked at my bag. 'Is that a bass?' Wide-eyed, he might have been asking if it were a mermaid, a unicorn, a pterodactyl. I told him the bass seemed to be locked in on the whitebait, so he might want to try a much smaller lure, something like a wee Toby. 'I haven't got one of those, I don't think anyone on my websites mentioned them.' I gave him a twenty gramme silver and white job (my desert island lure) and sat down for a smoke. Third cast and his rod bowed over with those slow hefty thumps that tell you it's a bass. It was one fat lady, maybe three-and-a-half pounds. That young chap was like the Cheshire Cat, whenever I walk past the outcrop I can still see the smile on his face.

One more caveat, people sometimes say my views are a bit tentative, that I reckon something, I believe something else, and there's not a whole lot that I really claim to know for sure. Fair comment. And no apology. I'm not a bass after all, just a chap with a fishing rod, so no certainties from my end, just opinions and experiences. But here's what I hope this book might do. I hope a few bass fishers – novices or old-stagers – will pick up some ideas that give them better outings and more fish, without a visit to the supermarket seafood counter, the poor-house, or the psychiatrist. Because helping someone land a decent bass, fritter away less money on tackle, or turn maddeningly grim fishing conditions into modest success, that's what I really enjoy.

And there lies the most important advice I'd offer to any fisher. Enjoy yourself. If some of my tips sound like fun, give them a go. If others would make your sessions less satisfying, ignore them. The best bass trip isn't the one that produces the most or the biggest fish, it's the one that produces the biggest grin and makes you want to get back out there as soon as possible.

It was one of those nights when nobody with any sense would go bass fishing. Early April, a small tide, a bright half-moon, and just a whisper of a wave. On the other hand I was wide awake at three in the morning. I took some lugworms from the fridge and a bag of squid from the deep-freeze. (Even in rotten conditions, you never know, and the idea of running out of bait is too hideous to contemplate.)

I headed down to my nearest beach. Walking to the water I used my torch in case the tide might have exposed any new snags. Experience has taught me that I can be relied on to find obstacles on the sand, usually by landing on my skinny backside. But no unexpected rocks, what I saw was a pair of gleaming eyes, then another pair. The beach was jumping with foxes. Now I often see foxes on the rocks fishing for crabs in the pools, but here were a dozen or so just faffing about on the high water line. I took a look at the sand at my feet: some weed, the usual depressing load of plastic waste, some odds and ends of commercial netting gear, and a whole lot of squid and rotting mackerel. A fishing boat must have been spring-cleaning its holds, dumping all the rubbish onto my beach and providing the local foxes with a rather smelly all-you-can-eat buffet.

I thawed my squid, on with a juicy one and I had a fish within minutes. Sitting on my backpack-stool in the moonlight I caught nine bass in two hours. And every time I turned on my torch to release a fish I saw the flashing eyes of four or five foxes twenty-odd yards behind me, watching intently. I tried tossing

*them a mangled squid, but there was no interest. I reckon they
were completely full and fancied no more than a bit of light
entertainment while their feast digested.*
So I sat there, a smiling fisher with his posse of smiling foxes.

A word on how things are organised. My ideas about bass are
in normal typeface like this: how I fish, why I think it works, the
advice I'd offer on conditions, tactics, lures, flies, bait, tackle, fishing
spots… I should mention that often I don't distinguish between
lure-fishing and fly-fishing. They're both ways of catching bass that
are feeding on small swimming creatures – fry, sandeels, prawns,
and so on. The only differences are the rod and reel you use and your
casting style; and the bass don't care about things like that.

Let me apologise up-front for my photos. I hope each of them
makes a useful point, but they certainly don't qualify as bass fishing
pin-ups. I'm too clumsy and inept to take my camera down by the
water in the dark, so my pictures are of fish I've brought home.
That's why they all look pretty much the same. I read articles by folk
described as fishing writers and photographers. I'm neither of those
things, I'm afraid, just a fellow who catches quite a lot of bass and
who'd like to pass on some of his ideas. By the way, all the catches in
my snaps and stories were within the legal limits at the time. When
I started writing this book, we were allowed to take any number of
bass above an absurdly-small minimum size and at any time of year.
As it goes to press, we are banned from keeping anything at all. We
can only hope the future will bring a sensible framework somewhere
between those extremes.

• For light amusement, pointless yarns and observations are in this
typeface (so you can skip over them without losing my drift).
Then there's the song quotations at the beginning of each
chapter. If you're curious you can look up the songwriters
responsible at the very end of the book. They're all songs I sing
while fishing. Bass are skittish but they're not put off by a loud,
untalented warbler who couldn't carry a tune in a paper bag.

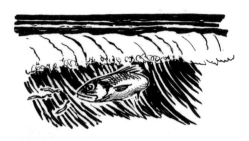

- Once in a while someone suggests I should be a bass guide: 'You catch a lot of fish, and you really like helping other people to catch, so why not?' And here's why not: because I can imagine nothing that would make me homicidally crazy faster.

  As a young man in West Africa I supplemented my modest salary by taking holiday visitors out on the rocks. I had some lovely clients, determined to enjoy themselves, interested in anything they saw, delighted with anything they caught. And I had some proper gits. If they landed a fish, this was down to their brilliance. If they didn't, I was a shite guide. If they lost a good one by trying to horse it in too quickly, my tackle was rubbish. And worst of all, I was stuck with them.

  These days I can give a fellow fisher a spot of advice, a lure, or some bait, then wander off along the shore and restore my peace and quiet. But when people pay for a four hour trip, you can't just drop them back at their cars after twenty minutes because they're obnoxiously snotty eejits who wouldn't catch a fish at feeding time in an aquarium.

  I have nothing but admiration for fishing guides, but I'll never be one again. Too much stress, which a poster in one of my employers' mailrooms defined as 'an overwhelming desire to punch the nose of some moron who thoroughly deserves it.' They had another poster which said, 'The beatings will continue until morale improves.' I liked that mailroom.

- I was on a soft sand beach at dawn when I heard a noise like a monstrous hailstorm. On with my torch, the shore was spattered with five-inch mullet. Right in the shallows two fat seals were lashing about like conger eels with kidney stones, making huge splashes to drive the mullet onto dry land. After a few minutes the seals flopped ashore and tucked in – but not before I'd

68cm (nearly 8lbs) from a decently stirred-up sea in late October. The wave looked frothy enough to colour the surf, so I started out with whole squid. Result: two tiddlers. I took a closer look at the water and found it was pretty clear, so I switched to a single 4/0 jammed with ragworms. As well as this one I released a couple of three to four pounders. Then I ran out of ragworms.

Moral: if it isn't working, change something. I reckon a good bass fisher's always wondering what to try next. Some people explain fishing success by talking about putting in the hours. Fair game, you don't catch bass from your sofa or your favourite bar-stool. But lots of hours fishing in the same unproductive way just lead to lots of very long disappointing trips.

filched a few live-baits. I'd love to learn how to throw a cast-net, but I reckon it would be easier to strike up a working relationship with a seal or two.

- I was driving to one of my beaches at about three-thirty in the morning when a police car raced up behind with the lights flashing. I pulled over and two young bobbies came alongside – all bobbies are young at my stage of life. 'Do you know what time it is?' 'More or less, after three, before four.' 'Have you been drinking?' 'I probably had a whisky last night.' 'Would you be prepared to take a breathalyser test?' At which point the second young chap shone his torch on the interior of my car. 'Don't bother with the breathalyser, Colin, he's a fisherman. He's not drunk, just daft.'

CHAPTER TWO

An Approach to Bass Fishing

A change is gonna come

When I run into early morning dog-walkers down by the water they frequently wind up saying something like, 'I should get my gear back out and have a go, but I don't have the patience for fishing.' Now I'm not an all-round fisher, just a bass fisher. I can't always tell a plaice from a flounder, rays give me the creeps, and I'm scared of conger eels and weevers, even little ones. And maybe chasing some of these species takes patience, but I reckon a patient bass fisher catches as much as a cross-eyed cricketer in handcuffs. Bass fishing's all about change, movement, experimenting, thinking. Sitting on a tackle-box watching tip-lights doesn't do the business, at least not reliably. Determination and adaptability are a help, patience can be a handicap.

Meet a fisher with a single bass in the bag and often this is what I hear: 'First cast, as it hit the water. Since then not a nibble.' My own experience backs this up, bites generally come quickly or not at all. And that tells us something. It says that if you're fishing in the right place in the right way, fish will be onto your bait or lure like a flash. Bass grow slowly, they need a lot of food to grow at all, so they don't hang about when they find what they're after, they latch onto it as fast as an accountant on a tax loophole or a terrier on a rat. And the flip-side's true as well. If you aren't having any joy, you're in the wrong spot, you're using the wrong fly, lure, or bait, or you're not fishing properly for the conditions.

- Have you noticed the way fishing tackle goes up in price if they can shove the word 'bass' into the product description? There's a lesson for us there. So does anyone want to buy a pair of second-hand bass fishing trousers, only slightly torn; or a nineteen year-old bass car, two not very careful owners?

- When a bite fails to develop, people say the fish must have felt the hook. Unlikely I reckon. Bass chomp up razor and mussel shells, so their mouths can't be very sensitive.

Late July, I had a sleep-in – by my insomniac standards – only arriving at my fishing spot a little before the dawn. There was a gentle onshore breeze and the water seemed fizzy enough to stir up a few sandeels, so I clipped on a mid-sized shallow-diver and let fly. Nothing doing, so a much slower retrieve, a sandeel with a dodgy work ethic. Again not a touch, but in the half-light I noticed a swirl behind my lure. I took a thinking break and sat on a boulder while I rolled a smoke. Watching the water I saw a huge slurp, then half a dozen whitebait leapt clear of the wave. I switched to a small Toby and I was straight into the fish.

A mid-summer morning and I'm fishing over high water on a shingle beach. The shingle gives way to a bunch of lugworm beds, so I'm casting to them and letting my bait trickle along in the tide. But it's as slow as a politician answering a straightforward question, all I've managed is two tiny schoolies.

12

Then it starts to get light, splashes right at the water's edge. After a quick polish of my specs I realise the splashes are sandeels, and there are some healthy swirls as well. Now I used to be a fair distance runner in my day, but sprinting along a pebbly beach in trouser waders is hard work, and I'm in a muck sweat by the time I get to the car. I wipe my face and glasses, grab my lure rod, clip on a skinny plug, and have another bash at the Usain-Bolt-in-a-vat-of-treacle routine. Back at the water's edge, scanning, walking, scanning. Then there's a walloping boil ten yards along the beach, maybe six feet out. A gentle lob-cast parallel with the wave, three or four turns of the reel, and everything goes crazy. I had four bass, the best right on four pounds, in under an hour. And I guarantee I'd have caught none of them if I'd stuck it out with the lugworms.

So a good motto for a bass fisher would be, 'If at first you don't succeed, don't keep doing what you're doing.' Change where you're fishing, or change how you're fishing. People sometimes explain a blank by saying, 'They just weren't there today.' Here's another, more hard-nosed version of that statement: 'I fished for four hours in the wrong place.' The bass were somewhere, they hadn't buzzed off to Ibiza for a weekend of loud music and recreational substance abuse. A less patient or more determined fisher at least would have tried to find them.

One reason so many bait-fishers don't go searching for their bass, I think, is that they burden themselves with too much gear. Lure-fishers tend to move a lot, often their tackle's just a rod and a knapsack. (Most of us carry more lures than we'll ever use, but a dozen twenty gramme plugs, spoons, and plastics don't make for a back-breaking kit-bag.) Beach-fishers on the other hand sometimes have two rods in a tripod, a box of rigs and weights to sink an ocean liner, a deck-chair, a flask of tea, cheese toasties, an umbrella, a microwave oven, a television set, and a Sky antenna dish. Or maybe not quite, but you get my point. By the time you've humped that lot along the beach and set up your Mount Everest base camp, you're not going anywhere, you're going to wait for the action to come to you. And that's not a great way to fish for bass. Myself, I hit the beach with more clobber than I used to and more than I'd like to. I carry a fair-sized backpack. There's not much in it, just a spare spool, a few hooks, some mono, a winder of ready-tied rigs, and a fleece. But the canny thing is that my pack doubles as a little stool, and my gammy leg means misery if I can't sit down. I also carry a sand-spike, not to hold the rod while I fish, but to lean it against while I bait up, change my weight or hook, roll a ciggie, or answer a call of nature. I suppose I could dump it, but I doubt I ever will.

Once I had to wade into a brutal surf to pull out an eejit who was drowning. My spike was my wading staff, and I have no doubt but that it saved two lives that day, one of them my own. So the sand-spike stays. Besides the bag and the spike I carry one rod, an eleven and a half footer that's light and easy in the hand. Bunking a mile down the beach to find a better wave isn't a problem. In the words of Pete Townsend, 'I'm mobile' (*Going Mobile*, Track Records, 1971). Roger Daltrey's a trout-fisher by the way, I'm sure he travels light as well.

• In the USA I understand the Coast Guard charges fees to people who need to be rescued. It seems like a good idea to me, and something the RNLI should consider, with the tariff on a sliding scale based on the level of stupidity of the folk who call them out. Bad luck or sudden change in the weather: free. Putting to sea in an unreliable boat: five hundred quid. Being cut off by a rising tide: two grand. Jumping off a pier: your wetsuit, car, and house.

• I was plugging in a cove on the north coast when I saw a crippled seagull. It was paddling through the wave about thirty feet from shore, trailing a broken wing and squealing. I thought the decent thing would be to end its suffering, so I tried to drag it in. My first fling was way off the mark, the lure caught by the breeze, so I switched to a wedge. As I was about to cast I saw a triangular fin, then a swirling splash and the gull was gone. Porbeagle ten yards from my boots. On another trip to the same cove I saw another porbeagle, this one just finning through the ripple, and again only thirty-odd feet away. Maybe someone should try tying a seagull fly.

• Some tackle is designed to catch fish, but product developers find it easier to run focus groups with fishers – and we'll buy almost anything.

We'd just had the first proper autumn hoolie, the surf was a pleasure, busy and foamy. But a blow after a calm often stirs up a slew of weed, and this one fit the bill to perfection. First cast, a dogged fight, and in came about twenty pounds of the vegetarian catch-of-the-day. I nipped off the hook-length, shouldered my bag, and set off along the beach. Every fifty-odd yards I chucked my weight into the waves to see if it would come back with a lump of wrack. On the sixth or seventh stop I was clear, so back to a proper rig, on with a whole squid, and in business.

Physical mobility's one thing. Just as important, a bass fisher needs to be flexible. Not in the yoga sense thank goodness, or my creaky joints would have me miles up the creek: I mean flexible about how to fish. If your casts aren't getting bites, try a different range. If your fly, lure, or bait's being ignored, use something else. And we all struggle with this because most fishers have our favourite approaches, usually ones that have done the job in the past. I know I fall into the trap. In a stirred-up sea I love a whole squid, and I sometimes stay with it longer than I should. Why? Because a lot of my better bass (over about eight pounds) have been on squid. In a millpond calm I'm addicted to a twenty gramme silver and white Toby or a white muddler minnow, because the little beauties have saved more blanks than anything else in my boxes. Along with my beloved woolly hat these things are my good luck charms. But to be a better fisher I ought to be less of a superstitious twit. I need to give the squid, Toby, or muddler its fifteen minutes of fame, and that's all. If it doesn't come up with the goods, I should drop it like a bad habit and try something else.

Another thing that's easy to do on unthinking auto-pilot is cranking a lure. My default setting's a brisk turn of the reel-handle every second or so, giving a slightly bouncy retrieve with a slinky ska rhythm. And it works pretty well – sometimes. When it doesn't deliver, I can be tempted to clip on something new or make a move. But before I do that I try to be firm with myself. Dump the Desmond Dekker beat and try a faster winding rate (the Buzzcocks), or a slower one (Percy Sledge). Often I find the same lure, fished differently, will turn up trumps; often but not always.

It was late May and the plugging had been good for a week. On every rising tide the cove had been filling up with finger mullet, followed by bass gorging on them. I'd taken a few home and their bellies had been stuffed with mullet to the point where I wondered they still were swimming, never mind feeding. A silver and black jointed plug, fished really slowly, seemed to drive them crazy. But not this time. About one cast in three got me a follow, but nothing was hitting the lure. OK, I thought, maybe early whitebait, on with a little Toby. Same story, follows but no pulls. A faster retrieve, then a slower retrieve, no difference. Got it, must be jelly-fry, time for a wee fly on a dropper. Follows, no pulls. In the end I decided to try everything in my box, every hard bait, every plastic. It was the eleventh and final lure that started me catching. I saved it till last because it's the goofiest piece of shite I ever saw, about six inches long, two semicircle hooks, fluorescent pink and yellow. I found it on a reef on a low spring tide. It had a Japanese name, so I reckoned it was an expensive number, but in the water I thought it looked about as appetising as a dog turd in a soup bowl. The fish disagreed, they absolutely loved it. I released five bass, then stuck one in the bag and went home. I cleaned my fish right away, expecting to find it had been feeding on something weird and exotic, maybe something pink and yellow. And its stomach was jam-packed with … finger mullet. Not for want of trying but that lure has never caught another bass.

- I knew a rescue helicopter pilot. In summer, when all the twits blow out to sea on air-mattresses or strand themselves as the tide comes in, he described his job as 'interfering with natural selection'.

One more thing, fish when the bass are active, not just when the weather's good and there's nothing much on the television. As a rule I find sunny day trips are a complete waste of time. I may see a few fish, I may even catch a few tiddlers, but the bigger bass don't show up often in conditions that call for sunscreen, flash dark glasses, and baseball caps with tackle company logos. Evenings-into-nights are good, and I reckon the sport picks up properly about an hour after dark. But I'd say the best time of all – with bait, fly, or lures – is the early morning, from a couple of hours before dawn through to the first rays of sun on the water. Bass feed all through the night, but they seem to feed hardest as it's coming to an end. Back a few years, the pubs used to shut at half-ten, and the bartender would shout 'Last orders' at ten-fifteen. That was when the serious boozers would chug like mad to get a couple more pints in before chucking-out time. I believe the end of the night works like last orders for bass, they have one final eating binge, filling their tummies while the going's still good.

Of course some fishers hate early starts, and I suppose they should stick to evenings – after all, fishing's supposed to be a pleasure, not a way of turning your alarm-clock into an instrument of torture. But even if you're an evening type, if you're not too chuffed with your catches, be flexible. Try staying later, starting earlier, just try something new.

And that's the approach. Don't be patient, be determined. If you're not catching, be ready to move to a different spot, to try another time or lure or retrieve or bait, to switch around almost anything. Watching a tip-light and hoping for a change of luck isn't real bass fishing. The old IBM slogan – 'Think' – is good advice. Unless the rod's bent all the time, think – where to go next, what change of bait might do the trick, what lure or fly. Or as Albert Einstein put it, 'Insanity: doing the same thing over and over again and expecting different results.' Wikipedia doesn't mention Albert as a bass fisher, but I'm sure he was. His hair, the only way you get hair like that is by standing on a beach in a gale.

I was on a north coast beach in mid-December. It didn't look promising, a small tide, a light breeze out of the north, and a touch of frost. But I'd driven fifteen miles so I was going to have a few chucks anyway. There wasn't much wave, but I know this beach well, there's always a decent surf at the eastern end. I hiked a mile through the sand, and sure enough there was my fizzy water, two or three sets of breakers, as bassy as you could wish. I was quite chuffed with that. 'Local knowledge strikes again,' I thought. But the bass were as impressed as a bunch of punk-rockers at a West End musical. Three casts at all distances from five to fifty yards and my ragworms were untouched. So where were the fish? The day before, I remembered, the wind had been easterly, and the old trout-fisher in me had a brainwave. An east wind would push the bass food – and the weed – to the western end of the beach. I hoofed it all the way back to where I'd started, where the wave was tiny. But yes indeed, there were a few mats of tangled wrack. Fishing about twenty feet from the start of the weed I managed two bass and a flounder.

Midwinter, we'd had a succession of gales and there was plenty of wave. The water was coloured, so I was using whole

unwashed squid, lots of juice and scent, but all I could catch
was whiting – which are a real pain when you have to tie up a
new bait with fingers like frozen chipolatas, all for a tiddler. So
I switched to razor clam, another good choice in gungy water.
First cast brought me two tiny schoolies, one on each hook. Then
I had four half-decent bass, all between two and four pounds, in
the space of about an hour. With my last razor clam gone it was
back to squid – and immediately I caught a micro-whiting.

• These days a good blow when the tides are jumping can mean days and days of weedy surf. It's pushed up to the high water line, then it sits there until a bigger tide pulls it all back into the wave again. When I was a youngster – fifty-something years ago, though I hate to say so – this didn't happen. After the first decent storm the farmers would swarm onto the beaches with their carts and their pitchforks, and the tide-line would be picked as clean as a hambone in a houseful of terriers. They used to leave the weed in the corner of a field, so the rain could leach the salt out, then use it as fertiliser. I was in a garden shop the other week and dried seaweed was on sale, fifteen quid for a small container.

A very last thought, no matter how long they've been at it, successful fishers are open-minded and utterly shameless about pinching ideas. Bass fishing's all about learning from experience. Your own experience is great. So's other people's. And as they say in academia, swiping information from one source is plagiarism, swiping it from lots of sources is research. The better your research, the more you catch, so it makes sense to pick up insights wherever you can, even – or especially – if they run counter to what you believe already. Poor fishers will say they know what they're doing, they'll keep doing it – patiently – whether it works or not. Better fishers realise that bass often spring surprises, so they aren't afraid to change their minds or their tactics.

High summer and I was on a Mount's Bay beach for the last of the ebb. It's a sandy beach, but at low water you're about ten yards from a dirty great lugworm bed and I was lobbing my worm baits into the magic spot. Except there wasn't any magic. One hour, three moves along the shore, and one bite – which felt like a flounderette with an eating disorder. Finally I had a sensible thump, a bass of about a pound-and-a-half. I waded into the shallows to release it. The fish wriggled in my hand, and I noticed a small sandeel flying from its mouth, then another wriggle and another sandeel. Had I been better prepared I'd have grabbed some frozen eels from my bag. Instead I had to leg it back to the car, swap rods, and start chucking sandeel shads and small plugs into the wave. I fished another hour for five good bass.

There are days when you know the fishing will be great, this was one of them. The surf was perfect, a warm onshore breeze and half a dozen rows of breakers bubbling over the sand. I was on a beach with a ton of lugworm beds and I could feel my weight skipping across the ridges where the worms are densest. But hardly so much as a nibble: one baby bass and a weever was all I managed in an hour and a half – and I like weevers as much as wheel-clampers. A hint of the dawn was in the sky, I reckoned I had an hour of fishing time left. So what to do? I loaded a 4/0 with head-hooked ragworms – which are as common on this beach as gluten-free Peruvian street-food stands – and lobbed out. Immediately I was into a fish, a three pounder. By the time the sun was glowing on the headlands I'd run out of ragworms and I'd lost count of the bass I'd returned. I know I kept three because I gave them to a friend who has a big family. I asked him to report on the stomach contents of the bass, hoping to solve this little mystery, but they were empty.

New Year's eve, there was a warm onshore blow gusting up to about thirty knots, a busy surf. I was on a beach that can *produce good bass in a decent wave, so I was chucking big squid into the fizz. But all I was catching was wee schoolies. Gorgeous baits, juicy enough to make a grown man drool, and the better bass weren't tempted. So where might they be? There's a rocky patch about thirty yards out from the low tide line, and I reckoned it was worth a shot. I tied up a new leader with a weak length to the lead. A forty yard fling, then I twitched the gear in until I felt a slight snag. Two minutes later the weight popped off and a five pound bass was doing its best to swim to America.*

- Fishers get narky about other fishers leaving rubbish behind, and so do I. But why's it worse to drop bait-wrappers and hook packets than beer tins and styrofoam cups? I suppose you could say that the fishing gang ought to be into conservation, that we

A full moon in late September, almost no wave. Walking along the beach I could see sandeels dimpling in the shallows. I spent forty-five minutes twitching a sandeel along the bottom for one baby conger. Then I tried a bunch of ragworms: eleven bass in an hour including the two above, best 62cm. Finally I chucked out a sandeel-type lure: a tiny pollack.

Even when it's blindingly obvious it isn't always right. There may or may not be a rule-book about how to catch them, but bass can't read anyway. Logical thought's a good starting point when you're wondering how to fish. If that doesn't do the job, it's time to start experimenting, to do something different.

As a friend used to say, 'There's a difference between perseverance and bloody-minded stupidity.'

should set an example and take really good care of the sea and the shore. And that's true. But I think there's a less noble reason for our indignation and outrage: we don't want the dog-walkers or the surfers to suspect that we were the selfish scumbags who dumped the fishing shite.

• I was fishing in Mount's Bay and at first light I saw another figure on the beach, a fellow carrying a tripod – but I couldn't see any rods. It turned out he was a professional photographer looking for a postcard shot of St. Michael's Mount at dawn. He came up to me and asked if I'd mind being in the picture, a lone figure against the orange glow of the sunrise. He offered me ten quid for my trouble, so I told him to donate it to the RNLI. Then the fun began. Could I move my bag and my sand-spike out of the shot as they broke up the line of the sand? Could I put my hood up, that would make me look mysterious? Could I give my trouser-waders a quick rub, they seemed to be coated with all sorts of gunk? Finally everything was to his liking and he beetled off to his camera position. 'Two steps to your left and about five metres into the surf if you can. Perfect.' Then I had a thumping bite – it was a fat three-pounder – and my new friend went crazy. 'Stop moving, stand still. Stop bending your fishing rod, I need a straight line to cut the horizon. Keep your left hand in your pocket and look bored. Stay where you are, don't walk up the sand. What is your problem?' By the time I beached the fish he'd gone. I've never noticed myself on the postcard stands, and I don't reckon the RNLI had its tenner either. Some folk sneer at models, but it isn't as easy as you might imagine.

• I read an article that said bass love ragworms. That's meaningless, like saying I love Buffalo chicken wings. I do, but I also love mackerel, burgers, spinach, tomatoes, pasties, bacon, bananas, toast … Bass eat almost anything that's in good supply.

CHAPTER THREE

Working Out How Bass Behave

...in the alley ...looking for food

No doubt about it, along with a pair of lucky socks this is the most important attribute of a successful bass fisher. If you can find feeding fish on a regular basis you'll catch more than your share. In classic conditions – bubbly breakers on a surf beach or a fizzy wave over a shallow rock mark – it may not be too hard to put yourself into a decent spot. But what about the poorer days and nights, the calms, the offshore hoolies, the times when the magic socks are in the laundry? You're not likely to catch as much on these trips, but if you think a bit harder about bass behaviour, I believe you'll be surprised how well you can do when other folk are going home in disgust. And here's a fact: bass need to eat, whatever the weather and the sea-state.

Finding feeding bass is all about knowing what drives them and how this will play out on the mark you're fishing. I think of it as local knowledge – often extremely local, working a bait into a tiny scour, casting a lure to a little outcrop, bringing a fly through a narrow channel – with a dollop of common-sense on top. The fashionable term's watercraft; probably because local knowledge sounds like the preserve of some scruffpot (like me) with a tatty rod and an evil-smelling rucksack; while watercraft might belong to the more elegant fisher so beloved of the tackle companies, with a Japanese lure outfit and a bum-bag full of twenty quid plugs. Either way we need to know what makes bass tick.

Sometimes I chat with other fishers and they tell me I think like a bass. It's meant as a compliment and I'm flattered, but it isn't true. I treasure the illusion that I'm quite a pensive type, but bass can't be said to think at all. They're simple creatures leading simple lives. Their genes drive them to breed as soon and as much as possible. To do that they have to grow as fast as possible and to survive as long as possible. And that's that. But for the fisher that's more than plenty.

• I went to take a look (with a rod, a proper look) at a popular beach. There was a handy carpark but I was shocked at the rates, four hours for four pounds eighty. So I left my car on a lane and had a bash. Next spring I went back to find a new parking tariff. Between ten at night and ten in the morning it was one pound twenty. I met a local fellow and commented on this. 'Oh yes, my handsome.' he said, 'Much too dear before. So those that live in the village, we put signs in our cars, 'Tried to pay but your machines are all mucked up." His language might have been a bit ruder than that, but his consonants were slurred by a mouthful of pasty, I'll give him the benefit of the doubt. 'OK, then what?' I asked. 'Well now, couldn't tell lies, could we? We had to muck up the machines good and proper. So we stuck a 3/0 hook in each of the coin slots. Then the chap that runs the parking, he had to pay the mechanic a hundred and fifty quid a time to get the hooks out. That's when he decided to charge us something sensible.' Cornish fishers, we may talk funny but we're not daft.

- Especially in dodgy conditions I check several meteorological websites, looking for one with a decent forecast. So when I come home like a rat that's been drowned in a wind tunnel I can say 'The weather people were wrong' instead of 'I went out in a howling toad-strangler because I'm nuts.'

Bass need to grow – the idea

This is the big one because it can tell us where the bass are likely to be and what they're likely to be eating. And I reckon you need to think of a bass as being the mirror opposite of a chubby human in the month of January. This is when the New Year's resolutions are still fresh, so our plump friend's determined to eat less and to take plenty of exercise. He sometimes makes an explicit accounting. 'I had a burger and a double whack of chips, I need an extra-long jog.' 'I did a ninety-minute training session with the rugby club, that entitles me to a large vindaloo and nine pints of stout.' It's a simple calculus, calories burned off through exercise against calories packed on at the table or the bar.

I've read articles describing bass as greedy or lazy. Not so, fish don't have undesirable character traits like people, but it's easy to imagine they do. Because a bass behaves like our dieter – only in reverse. Chubby-chap wants to lose weight, whereas the bass needs to bulk up as quickly as possible. Size will help it to survive and breed, so the fish is hard-wired to put on body-mass.

Our lumpy human tries to balance jogging against chips, and a bass is similar – but back-to-front, the bass wants more calories taken in, less burned off. And a big bass grows slowly, swims laboriously, and converts protein inefficiently; so it needs a lot of surplus calories, more than most other predators. It can't afford to forage far and wide or to chase hard-to-catch prey. Instinct tells it to find as much food as it can while expending very little energy indeed. This means a good feeding zone will have plenty of stuff to eat, and that stuff will be easy to get hold of – a very specific pair of demands.

Think about a shoal of mackerel. There's lots of food there, fattening food as well, oily fish with plenty of calories. But bass rarely seem to attack shoals of mackerel. Why? I'd say it's because mackerel are fast and manoeuvrable. A bass large enough to swallow a decent mackerel is a lumbering brute, it's going to use up more energy chasing down its prey than it would take on by eating it. Divers tell me they see big bass with mackerel shoals, but the bass lie in the water just beneath the feeding frenzy, sucking up the smashed and crippled baitfish that the mackerel miss. That's a ready-meal, a self-service seafood carvery, very few calories consumed in running it down. And dead mackerel, whole or in bits, take no catching at all, which is why a head-and-guts is such a good bait near fishing harbours in the summer.

But live mackerel's a great bait for bass too, how does that fit with this notion? Well, a live-bait isn't nearly as quick and nimble as a free-swimming fish. It's tethered and sometimes weighted down as well, so the hunter has far less work to do for its meal than if it were zipping around in a shoal. Bass aren't politically correct, their watchword is, 'Look out for the handicapped. Then eat them.'

And even shoaling mackerel sometimes come in for a hammering. There's a lure mark I fish where the tide runs in a narrow channel between the shore and a rocky outcrop. When the current's strong I see bass pouncing on joey mackerel as they battle the wild swirls. Again these are easy pickings. The bass can lie at the edge of the rip, in a gentle drift, then chomp down a tide-battered fish that's as helplessly disoriented as a Cornish tractor-driver going round and round Piccadilly Circus.

Sandeels are another example, rich and greasy, a prime source of energy for a growing bass. But sandeels are agile chaps, zigging and zagging at high speed in open water. And that's why skinny lures, big flies, and sandeel baits can work so well around dawn and dusk, times when the wee fellows bury themselves in the sand and emerge from their burrows. This is when they're vulnerable, a bass can hoover them up while they're dithering about, neither swimming flat-out nor safely tucked away. No chasing a nimble little fish through the ocean wave, just a relaxed swim in the shallows, picking up preoccupied sandeels the way our overweight friend might pick up tempting treats from a buffet table.

• Catch a whopper and a lot of folk will dismiss it: 'You were just in the right place at the right time.' True, but you only find the right place by knowing your marks. And you're more likely to be out at the right time if you fish a lot.

Then think about razor clams. They're rich as well, and a large razor's a healthy mouthful even for a big bass. But bass only really seem to feed on razors after a storm. And why? Because catching them from their burrows would take a lot of swimming about, followed by a tug-of-war. On the other hand a big wave turns them into readily edible flotsam, washing about in the surf like dumplings in a soup-bowl.

And here's the best bit, the instinct that drives fish to scoff a good deal more energy than they burn off shows up most strongly in bigger bass. A tiddler can dart about like a mad thing, picking up the odd worm in its travels, because it takes very few calories to move it from A to B. But a hefty old female, the kind we like to catch, must be more selective, because driving five (even ten) pounds of bodyweight through the water takes a lot more effort. Lunker bass are like our bulky human after the rugby session, in the mood for a feast, and not prepared to do any more than smile at the waiter and ask for another giant helping of onion bhaji.

27

Further evidence of this need for tons of easy food comes if you clean a big bass. Mine generally contain fish, and they're always slow-moving bottom-huggers. Rockling, flounders, and weevers are commonest, chunky meals the bass can catch without much chasing. Schoolies often are rammed with whitebait, but the fat ladies don't mess with nifty nibbles unless they're crippled or dead, they prefer the sluggish lumps. Lure-jockeys will tell you lots of mackerel and baby bass mean you're cranking too fast for an energy-conserving predator that refuses to burn calories on a sprint – slow down to the speed of a gently swimming feast-hunter. And serious bait-fishers use serious baits. People look at my hearty hook-loads and ask me if I'm after sharks. No, but a beefy bass is going to invest some work swimming even a few yards to grab my offering, so I want to be sure there's a really good return on its investment, enough nourishment to make that effort worthwhile.

Of course bass being contrary, there are exceptions. Even whoppers sometimes have guts full of sand-hoppers, jelly-fry, or weed-maggots, morsels smaller than my fingertip. But there's an explanation: these creatures appear in swarms, like biblical plagues. So all the bass need do is to swim along with her mouth opening and closing, the goldfish on Valium routine. Food for just about zero caloric effort, a good way to put on weight. Luckily bass feeding on sand-hoppers are suckers for lugworms, and a pale seatrout fly or muddler minnow offers a decent imitation of a jelly-fry. Weed maggots are tougher, but a grub-like fly sometimes does the trick. And often the maggots attract mullet, so it's worth trying a lure that suggests a finger-sized mullet.

- I'm amazed how many water bottles I find on the shore. Who's spending money on this stuff, it sometimes costs more than beer? Anyway I knew a Canadian who started a bottling business. I don't recall the company name, but the slogan was something like 'Canadian Bottled', and the adverts had pictures of lakes, brooks, and so on. I asked my pal about it. Yes of course it was bottled in Canada. OK, where, a spring, a glacier? Oh no, an industrial estate by Toronto airport. People lapped it up, imagining it came from some virgin wilderness – and it was tap-water. All you needed was to buy a bottle, then keep filling it at your sink. Less waste that way as well, a container-for-life.

Bass need to grow – where to fish, what bait, fly or lure

So how does this idea about large scale effortless eating help us find more bass – ideally big ones? Well, it provides a good deal of what we need to know. It tells us when and where to fish, and what bait, fly, or lure's most likely to deliver.

First when to fish, and for me this one's a no-brainer. Your best chance of good bass fishing comes at times when more sensible folk are tucked up in bed. A lot of bass-food's easier to catch by night, like worms and crabs; and some nutritious prey species, like sandeels, at the changing of the light. Things that might put bass off their grub – seals, porbeagles, dog-walkers who hurl tree-trunks into the surf, bellowing buffoons on jet-skis – tend to lie low when it's dark. So it makes sense to chase bass when their dinner table's most fully laden and when there are least things to disturb them as they feed.

It's possible to catch big bass in daylight, especially in grey weather and a big surf. But the old saying's true, anything's possible until the probable gets in the way, and the odds are stacked heavily in favour of the nocturnal fisher. From a seat-of-the-trouser-waders calculation I'd say I have ten times as many takes in the darkness or half-darkness as I do in full light – and this applies to fly-fishing, lure-fishing, or chucking bait into the wave. I like a moonless night best of all, but only by a whisker, and even a clear sky with a blazing full moon knocks spots off a sunny morning.

A lot of successful fishers head out just before sundown and fish on into the black night. I prefer to show up a few hours before the first glimmer of dawn and fish through until sunrise. Partly this is because my spots are less crowded in the wee hours – generally I'm the only daft-head out and about at three o'clock on a summer night. Partly it's because I'd rather end my session in daylight than in pitch darkness. And mostly it's because I believe bass feed hardest at the end of the night, stoking up thoroughly for the long sunlit hours that lie ahead. Either way, whether you focus on evenings or on mornings, proper bass fishing will not be without a few sacrifices. Pub time, telly time, duvet time, something has to give.

- Bass feed on so many things I love to eat myself: crab, squid, mackerel, mussel, razor clam, prawns. Maybe I should be brave and try a few ragworms.

A warm night in July, an onshore breeze, I was on the beach at three. As I arrived I ran into two tourists who were leaving. They'd been fishing since eleven for one baby bass. When they found out I was a local they decided on a few more casts: 'If you think this is the time, we'll see if you're right,' uttered with the sceptical tone you'd expect from a VAT inspector with a nasty hangover. First cast and my ragworms produced a three pounder. Then a shout, 'I'm in.' And another, 'Me too.' After a couple of non-stop hours I headed home with a good eating bass. 'How did you know when they'd come on?' asked one of the chaps. I was tempted to invent something – KernowBass-dot-com, MagicLug-dot-co-dot-uk – but they might have believed me.

Now for the where to fish, and let's start with a situation we all run into, though not as often as we'd like: a biggish tide and a frothy surf at the start or end of an onshore blow. Four sets of waves are rolling onto a gently shelving shore-line – or maybe a flat one. A lot of fishers avoid a flat sea floor. 'Even with a long cast,' they say, 'my bait or lure will be in such shallow water. How can I expect a big bass in eighteen inches?' But that's the point. The tidal pull and the surf provide the food – worms and clams washed from the sand, stirred-up sandeels, crabs flipping in the tow, dead fish and squid being pushed inshore – and the combination of wave and shallowness helps the bass feed with very little effort.

The wave stirs things up and knocks seven bells out of the prey species – but not the bass. Bass, especially big bass, can deal with a brutal surf. I often catch chunky fish from the sort of sea that would scare the neoprene pants off most surfers, that would smack their boards onto the sand and suck the battered remains out into the mid-Atlantic. Even when a wired lead's being yanked from the bottom, when you have to scoot up and down the strand like a triple-jumper with the hiccups just to keep a tight line, fish keep feeding. I reckon this is because waves produce a pull-and-push effect, pretty well straight in and out from the shore, and hefty bass just go with the flow.

In a tidal rip they swim hard to stay in one place, but they don't seem to fight the shove and tug of the surf. On windless days I sometimes watch bass from the cliffs over one of my beaches. In a good swell I see big ones washing in towards the sand and back out again, drifting like lumps of weed, not expending any energy trying to swim against the surge. So even a raging sea can provide comfortable foraging for a fat fish.

Now for the shallow water part of the story. Shallow water makes food-gathering easier for predators and scavengers because it lets them hunt in two dimensions rather than three. In a deeper area, as the treats swirl around in the wave, our bass needs to search forwards and backwards, left and right, and up and down as well. It's like looking for a needle (or maybe a set of car-keys, I can't imagine why we'd care about a needle) in a haystack. The wretched keys could be anywhere, end to end, front to back, and top to bottom. But if the distance from top to bottom of the haystack were just one or two feet, we'd find the keys a whole lot faster. It's the same for our bass. In the shallows she has no need to search high and low for her next meal because there's only a few inches of water between them.

Late October and I was fishing a south-facing beach after a few days of southerly winds. The wave was a thing of beauty, four or five sets of three foot breakers, frothy water as far as the eye could see. And the wrack on the high-water line was spotted with bass treats – squid, mackerel frames, cuttlefish, crabs. So out went a whole squid on a couple of 4/0 hooks. But there was a snag (Murphy's Law states that there's always a snag) in the shape of a ton of weed, ugly great fronds of the stuff. I wandered along the beach hoping to find a clear spot. Every fifty-odd yards I made a cast then waited to see whether my gear had landed in a lump of kelp.

Finally I had a lob that didn't snag, but by now I was at a spot where the beach is totally flat. Indeed a surfer on his way home from clubbing came to see how I was doing. 'I don't know why you bother casting,' he said with an oddly fixed grin, 'just drop your bait. It's a foot deep everywhere.' He might have been out of his head on horse tranquilisers, but he was dead right. As we were chatting I felt a soft knock, a pause, then a hint of slack line. I walked up the beach to tighten and everything came to life. After a couple of thumping runs the fish began to weaken and I pulled her in. About ten yards out she became stranded, beached on a slight rise in the sandy bottom. I waded in and grabbed her. Just under eight and a quarter pounds. I had two smaller bass from the same thin water before the light came up.

So shallow water's a plus, at least in the hours of darkness. Often it's also a plus to fish close in. Again think from the point of view of this simple being, which needs to eat as much as it can without swimming too far or too hard. Where's the food likely to be thickest on the ground? A decent wave pushes everything – lost lobster-pots, jetsam from litter-lout mariners, seaweed, clams and mussels, worms, dead fish and squid, crabs – onshore. And where there's plenty of food, that's where the bass are most likely to be. Of course how close in can't be reduced to a formula, it depends on conditions. In general I like to fish in the fizziest, swirliest areas – more of a stir-up means more bass grub and easier hunting; and on average across all sorts of sea-states my most productive range is between five and thirty yards from the water's edge. In a tiny wave I've taken decent bass eighteen inches from the margin, in a scary Atlantic swell I've caught forty or fifty yards out. But for a lot of fishers this is the message: the bass – especially the better bass – probably are closer in than you think, and a lot closer than some of the experts would have you believe. I just glanced at one of the angling magazines which advised standing waist-deep in the surf and casting. At my favourite spots anyone standing that far out would need to cast towards the shore – and to give it some welly.

Mid-July, I was on a Mount's Bay surf beach at three in the morning, fishing lugworm at about twenty yards. It wasn't a spectacular session – the tide was small and the surf was a good bit lighter than I like – but I managed three baby bass and a four pounder in the first hour and a half. There were lights at the far end of the beach, then they came my way. Two holiday-makers, they'd been at it all night for a miniature flounder. I watched one of them make a cast and I'm bound to say I was impressed. It looked as if his lead might have wound up in America – but not among the bass. Now it's difficult to tell another fisher that he's doing it all wrong without sounding like an irritating smarty-pants television pundit, so I tried to be a bit of a diplomat. 'They seem to be really close in at the moment,' as if this were a surprise, 'maybe twenty yards out.' The visitors looked at each other and I could see what they were thinking: 'Bloody Cornish comedian taking the mick out of the Emmets.' Then one of them reeled in and re-baited with a healthy bunch of ragworms. He was using one of those enormous continental rods, maybe seventeen feet long, and he held it out in front of him as he dunked the worms in the water to toughen them up. 'Twenty yards? You're telling me you caught that fish twenty yards out?' I was just about to answer when the rod almost flew out of his hands. He was into a half-decent bass, between two and three pounds, at a range of seventeen feet. I suspect he's a believer now.

Early July and flat as a dab. It felt like one of those days that we Cornish pretend are typical summer weather, when the sun's almost uncomfortably warm once it rises. (In fact this happens about three times per decade, but keep it under your hat, we need the tourists.) Anyway I took my lure rod down to a cove not far from my house. Coming up to high water it's a boulder beach with a strong cross-flow. I arrived an hour before first light and immediately I could hear swirls and splashes. I sat down at a respectful distance from the sea and watched in the moonlight. There was a blanket of rotting weed on the high-tide mark, and shoals of finger-sized mullet were browsing their way along it, almost certainly picking off weed-maggots.

Then every so often a bass-sized boil. To attract a fish so close to the margin I needed a lure that would just sit in the water with the odd twitch to give it life – there was no way to retrieve through the fishy area without snagging the weed bank or standing so close as to scare everything away.

On with a black and white weedless and weightless soft plastic stick-bait, and I lobbed it from about twenty feet back. Plop, sink, tweak. By the time I almost could see into the water I'd had three bass between two and three pounds. Then I noticed headlamps thirty feet to my right: two fellows who might have stepped out of a tackle-shop commercial, with red rods, breathable stocking-foot waders, and just about everything that opens and shuts. It seems that once you've spent a couple of hundred quid on spiffy waders you feel the need to wade. So these two tromp out into the briny and start hurling poppers at the horizon. Only when one of them filled his boots

*(even fancy ones don't keep you dry when you fall over) did
they come back to the shore. Then I could point out that they'd
been fishing well outside the feeding area. They didn't have any
soft plastic lures – just the expensive stuff, Patchinko, Komono,
Flash Minnow, Gunfish – so I gave them a couple. Good
sports too, the one who'd gone for an impromptu dip hung up
his trousers on a rock and fished on in red underpants. They
caught some bass as well, from an area of water they normally
would have waded straight past.*

*There's an estuary I visit, usually when there's no surf on
either coast, when there's too much wave for safety, or when
my lure spots are slathered with as much weed as a sushi
bar on a night when the fish-lorry broke down. Now when you
think of an estuary you might have something in mind like the
Teign or the Tamar. And my estuary isn't in the same league. It's
where a tiny brook creates a sandy and weedy pool on a beach. It
fishes best around low water, so I take myself down for the couple
of hours around first light and the turn of the tide.*

*Over the years I've had a few bass there on surface lures
– not poppers, something small and discreet that slides across
the top – but I prefer to fish it with the fly. Not because I rate
any type of fishing as superior to any other, I don't. In my book
purists and fishing snobs are as entertaining as re-runs of party
political broadcasts. No, I like the fly-rod for my estuary-in-
miniature because it's the best way to cover the water, which
is between nine and eighteen inches in depth. I'm no distance
caster, but with a floating fly line, a six foot leader, and a little
white muddler minnow, I can work my way through every little
gully and past every weed-bed without fear of snagging up. It
isn't a way to catch big bass – though once I fluked a six pounder
– but it can be great fun. In such thin water even a schoolie's
preceded by a dirty great bulge, and there's nothing quite like
watching this bow-wave charging at the fly.*

- My mother swam almost year-round. One winter's day a naval helicopter tried to rescue her. She had the devil of a job to persuade the crew she wasn't drowning. She had a pretty loud voice, but nothing to match those rotors.

- I wonder if there's a word to describe an irrational fear of weever fish. Trachnidaphobia sounds good. By the way, weevers have no swim-bladders.

Now I strongly suspect that a lot of folk would feel a bit ridiculous lobbing their bait or lure just twenty-odd yards into the wave, then fishing in one or two feet of water – especially if they've spent years belting it out beyond the third or fourth or final breaker. And feeling ridiculous isn't helpful when you're trying to catch bass. If you think you're wasting your time, fishing in a dead zone, then likely you'll fish like an eejit. You'll unwrap a giant pasty, shove your beach-rod onto a tripod, and forget about it.

Even if you're using a lure or a fly, your mind will wander. Then you'll miss those quick thump bites and you'll curse like a pirate who's run out of rum and developed a nasty migraine at the same time. So here's a way to let yourself gently into the close range approach to beach-fishing without denting your confidence.

Start off with what you see as a normal cast, be it fifty-odd yards, the third wave, as far as your little arms will chuck it, whatever. Let the gear settle, wait five minutes. Then wind in about one-fifth of the length of your cast. Five more minutes, repeat the dose. You may be surprised how often you have a decent pull when you're thinking that your swivel's about to hit your end-ring. With a lure or a fly I always fish all the way in to the shore, and I often have a good hit within a couple of rod-lengths of my feet.

It was late April and I was on a soft sand beach that can work the oracle around low tide. It's a spot that crunches to the sound of razor clam shells and it produces gilthead bream

*as well as bass, especially in late spring. I arrived two hours
before first light which was to be about the same time as low
tide. (I can't help myself, when I know I'm off to fish a different
spot I always wake up too early.) Now this beach changes a good
deal, like a supermarket where they keep moving the stuff you
want into another aisle, but typically there are a few sandbars
with gullies between them. Not knowing where the gullies might
be, I put on a big razor bait and slung it out about fifty yards.
Dead as a dodo drumstick, so I wound in ten yards and waited
five minutes. Another ten yards, wait again. Then again. And
by now, with the dropping tide, I was thinking I must be fishing
almost on dry land. Then a solid thump and a yard of slack. A
two pound schoolie, released. So a new bait and a twenty yard
lob. A three pounder, released. And with the first gleam in the
sky, a three pound gilthead, dinner. Then a small schoolie. Once
it was fully light I made another twenty yard lob and watched for
the splash of the sinker. I was fishing in a tiny scour on top of a
sandbank, in about nine inches of water.*

*May, weeks of settled weather and a thrice-blasted easterly
breeze, then at last came a beach-fisher's forecast: south to
south-west, three or four, occasionally five or six, fair, but very
poor in rain squalls. The first proper blow after a calm spell
often hits the spot, so I thawed a bag of squid overnight and at
three o'clock the next morning I headed for the beach; where
my first thought was, 'Be careful what you wish for.' The wind
was onshore and it was pushing in at about fifty miles per hour,
fifty-five in the gusts. I'm not a muscular type and not a brilliant
caster, so I wondered whether I'd be able to chuck my gear into
the water at all, or whether it would fly back up the strand. One
way to find out, I put on the biggest squid in the packet, tied it
up with elastic thread, and gave it a hurl. I could feel the braid
peeling off in the approved manner, then it stopped dead, caught
by the howling gale. It was a very wet gale as well, so I turned my
back to the water to avoid being stung by high-speed rain pellets;*

and I wondered if my wife might be right and I might be totally barking. But no surprise, most fishers are a few coupons short of a pop-up toaster. After ten minutes I felt a hefty knock, pause, another knock, and then my gear took off for the mid-Atlantic. A nine-and-a-half pound bass.

I fished on until first light for a five-ish pounder and a few missed bites just so I could see how far I'd been casting. When I put my back into it I was managing twenty yards, mostly thanks to the wind resistance of the squid. That was putting me into the middle of the second breaker, which was crashing like a dodgem-car with an angry psychotic at the wheel, and where good bass were feeding anyway.

- A fresh limpet looks like a tasty treat. Never judge a mollusc by its cover.

So shallow water and short casts can help you put your bait, fly, or lure into those places where bass feast away without too much effort. And here's another thing, try to fish not just in a decent area but in exactly the bass buffet hot-spot. This is where local knowledge becomes very local indeed.

I spent (wasted, if you prefer) a lot of years chasing trout with a fly-rod in my hand. I never quite took to the big reservoir game which seems to be based on slinging out a huge, embarrassingly garish lure, then stripping it in by waving your hands like a hyperactive thrash metal drummer. I preferred fishing streams and small lakes, which is much more pensive, measured, and visual. Indeed other fishers sometimes were amazed when they looked in my bag. 'How come you caught some? You never seem to fish at all, you just stand there staring at stuff.'

Not far wrong either: I spent a lot more time scanning the water than casting at it. I was trying to pinpoint a likely-looking trout hangout in the stream, evidence of fish moving in the lake, the edge of a wind-lane where nymphs and emerging insects pile up, an overhanging tree with beetles falling into the drink. Then when I saw a promising spot I'd make one or two flicks.

The same approach seems to work when I go after bass with lures or the fly. In a rocky cove or a shallow sea-pool I don't believe that feeding fish are going to be scattered randomly. There tend to be sweet spots – what the trout-fisher would call lies – where predators hole up or make frequent visits, and these bass-lies can be very small indeed, often no bigger than a dustbin-lid.

So what makes a good bass-lie? No surprise, it's a spot where bass have access to plenty of food and where they can grab that food without a whole lot of swimming about. In a strong tide-flow, bass will hold station in a place that offers some shelter from the current – just like a trout in a stream – and a clear line of sight to the swirlier water. On windless days I've watched them doing exactly this, loitering in the lee of a rocky outcrop or a clump of wrack, where they can stay in position with just the odd flick of fin or tail. When a few baitfish go past, tumbling helplessly in the current, the old bass pounces, then back into the calmer spot to wait for the next snack. It's as if the tidal flow or the shove of the wave is a Yo Sushi style conveyor-belt pushing food along. And the bass, rather than fighting to swim against the conveyor-belt, sits in her lie watching it, then swoops when the time is right, when the sandeel roll or the mackerel sashimi trundles by.

• In really dire conditions there are two stories that keep me smiling. One's of a boatman who took my family fishing out of Dungarvan in the 1960s. If the wind was screaming across the bay – usually with squalls of rain – Declan would turn into the weather and say, 'It would be a grand day for the sailing.'

    The other's of the late Fred J. Taylor who was fishing with the late Richard Walker on a beastly cold river bank. After a while Taylor turned to Walker and said, 'I'll be glad when I've had enough of this.'

- Little bass travel in schools. That makes sense to me: when you hunt in a pack you can cover a wider area. But the monsters seem to be lone wolves. Just an idea, but I reckon it's because they can't afford to share their grub with other bass, they need to eat everything they find.

Of course Murphy's Law demands a problem and here it is: my trout outings were in daylight, but I do a lot of my bass fishing before the sun's up, which means I can't spot the likely-looking areas. Even with a full moon it's hard to work out what's happening beneath the surface more than a few yards away. Almost everything looks like a double-figure monster slashing at baitfish. Then I cast to it and find it's a tangle of weed moving in the wave, a dead gull, a chunk of driftwood, or a swimsuit abandoned by someone who underwent a speedy conversion to nudism. So I need to know my marks really well from visiting them in full sun – or as full as we get in this often dreary beach holiday capital of the UK. And when it's light I'm looking for places where food will be washed along in the wave or the current and concentrated into a narrow conveyor-belt, and where there's some sheltered water for the bass to lurk. A gap between a couple of obstructions – sometimes tiny obstructions, breadbin-sized or smaller – will do fine; or a gully in the shape of an hourglass, fat-thin-fat, so the predators can rest up in the gentler drift of the fat area; or a promontory that sticks out into the tidal flow; or a clump of kelp that breaks up the pushing of the waves. Man-made obstacles work just as well as natural ones: groynes, pilings, surface-water pipes, and so on. Channels, harbour-mouths, and pools can be productive as well. You just need to seek out places where the food swirls in and out with the tide, and where there's some calmer water close by to provide a comfy pig-out site for a waiting bass or three. When you find something that looks like a good ambush point, it's amazing how tightly the fish will hold into their magic spots. Cast too far to one or other side of the target and you'll be fishing the dead sea on a very wet Wednesday. Bring your lure or fly right through the middle of it, that can be a different story.

Early August when the sands are jam-packed with holiday-makers all day long. We'd had a few days of warm, still weather, there was no wave on any of my spots, so I headed for a boulder-strewn cove about an hour before the dawn. There'd been lots of sandeels in the water of late, so I started off with a slim, silvery-green shallow-diving plug on a slow retrieve, casting into the tide-swirls around the biggest of the underwater boulders. By first light I'd managed three bass up to about three pounds. Then a young chap showed up. He was on holiday from the Netherlands and he'd been fishing his way along the shoreline, but all he'd caught was a suicidal pollack of about half a pound. What, he wondered, was he doing wrong? I took a look at his lure, a sandeel-shaped shallow-diver, no problem. 'Try this,' I told him, 'see that big round rock sticking up? Cast about ten metres to the right of it.' Which he did, with the accuracy of a portly darts player on the television, but without any bass action. No surprise, this first cast was a dry run to see if his lure went where it was told. 'OK, now see if you can drop it one metre to the left of the rock and about one metre further out.' The cast, the plop, then a sudden swirl as a two pound bass grabbed his plug. (Of course it doesn't work out that well very often, but you feel like a genius when it does.)

Towards the end of October and there was a decent surf running on most of my favourite beaches. But thanks to the well-known Law of Murphy I'd just come home from a long work trip overseas and I had nothing at all to use as bait. (Since that day I've never left home without making sure there's a packet of squid, some sandeels, and a few razor clams in the deep-freeze.) But after two weeks away from the sea, nothing was going to stop me. I took my spinning-rod and went for a wander on a two mile shingle beach which has a few surface-water drain

41

pipes running across it. I clipped on a greeny-white sandeel shad and set off along the shore, casting into the wave and bouncing the lure through the surf-table. My third cast came up with a schoolie; then an even smaller bass, a nursery-schoolie or a play-groupie, half the size of the legal limit. So I lengthened my stride and headed for the first of the drain pipes, where the water was bubbling away as the swells and the tide-flow were broken up by the barrier. My shad splashed about eighteen inches down-tide of the pipe, and straightaway everything went solid. 'Rats,' I thought, 'I must have snagged the weed growing on the drain.' Then the weed shook its head and made for the horizon. It was a four pound bass. I fished the whole length of the beach that morning. Between the pipes I had four tiny basslets and two small flounders. At the pipes, three decent fish, nothing under three pounds.

So that's lure-fishing and the fly, where the closer you cast to the bass-lie, the better you'll tend to fare. Beach-fishing with bait follows a similar pattern, I find, with very specific spots on the sand throwing up a lot more fish than others. And this is something that came to me pretty late in my education as a bass fisher. I'd always supposed that surf-feeding bass would patrol their way steadily along the shore, back and forth like sentries on parade. I knew it was important to find the right range and that was as far as I went. But I've changed my thinking: not so much like sentries on parade, more like rugby-players on a pub-crawl. Pub-crawlers don't move steadily – even when they're sober. They duck into a pub, relax over a drink or so, then move swiftly to the next pub. Travel time's kept to a minimum so boozing time can be maximised.

And I believe bass on a beach are similar. Even on what looks like a pretty uniform expanse of sandy-bottomed surf there are areas where food piles up – the bass pubs – and areas where there's not much going on – the walks between pubs. Sometimes the pubs are obvious. There's a south coast beach where the sand often forms a series of ridges and gullies twenty feet across, running down the shore and into the water. The middles of the gullies are where stuff collects on the bottom, be it weed, dead sandeels, cuttlefish, or holiday-makers' lost sandwiches, sunhats, and socks. So no mystery, feeding bass are going to spend most of their time in these accumulations of food and flotsam.

But what about the really flat-looking beach where there are no features to be seen? If you take a wander through the shallows of even the flattest beach, you soon realise it's not as flat as you thought. Try it in wellies and you'll feel the ups and downs for sure. One step has the briny up to your ankles, the next has your boots full of water. And even the smallest dimple in the sand is a magnet for drifting bits and pieces. A dip a couple of inches deep and no bigger across than a dinner plate will hold shells and crabs, while the higher area around it's barren. And I'm convinced that feeding fish cover a beach by moving from one dip (or gully, or scour-out, or bass pub) to the next, like a rugby team on a jolly. They check out a feasting hole, sink a couple of squid or worms or dead fish, then on to the next bass-boozer.

So how do you find these fishy depressions? They can be really wee, and on most beaches they move from one tide to the next. Even if you could pinpoint a few in the afternoon, and even if your casting were accurate enough to land a bait in something the size of a frying-pan, by the evening tide the frying pan likely would have shifted.

Here's where the right gear can help. A lot of fishers I meet use hefty wired leads, their baits stay wherever their casts touch down, anchored snugly to the bottom until the fisher or a bass pull them free of their moorings. But if you fish the smallest sinker possible, with nothing at all to pin it to the sand, then your gear's going to move around in the wave and the tide; and like the crabs and sandeels and lost socks, it's going to find its way into the troughs and dimples. The weight has to match the state of the surf and the strength of the tidal pull. What I look for is the lightest lead that will almost – but not quite – hold bottom. I don't want it moving non-stop, that would make life pretty tedious and my gear would wind up at my feet in a big hurry. So it should stay put most of the time, then do a little skip-and-jump every time a bigger-than-average wave comes in.

Because I fish the early mornings so much, I tackle up before I hit the beach. I decide the night before where I think I'll be heading and what bait I'll start out with. That way I can have my leader tied on and ready to go, a single hook for a bunch of ragworms, a two hook rig for whole squid or razor clam, whatever. But the sinker doesn't go on until I'm right at the water's edge, quivering with anticipation like a skinny short-haired pointer as I size up the surf. In a typical three to six foot wave I'll kick off with a four ounce bomb. A smaller wave just means a smaller bomb, going down to a one-ouncer in a wussy little ripple. Obviously the waves sometimes are bigger than three to six feet, sometimes they're coming in like the sides of stately homes, and that means I'm not going to be able to hunt out the bass pubs. I'll just have to grit my teeth, put on a wired lead, and make the best of it. But I always use wandering gear if I can, it's the best way to find the feeding bass.

July, I meet up with another fisher in the beach carpark. He's read my catch reports and he wants to see how I deal with a small surf. I should never take folk fishing. I do it very rarely, for two good reasons. First, I spend half my time wondering how my temporary chum's getting on, so I don't concentrate properly. Second, often I catch nearly all the fish – then I feel like a jammy so-and-so and a failed guide to boot. Anyway we walk down to the water and it's a decent-ish wave, so I decide on a three ounce sinker and a cast of about twenty yards. The other fellow says he'll follow suit. Out goes my gear, and I can feel the lead making little skips every so often. Perfect, it's holding in a depression, then washing out and wandering on to the next depression. In quarter of an hour I have a three pounder. 'How far out?' 'Twenty yards. On rag.' Another wee while, a smaller one. 'Same range?' 'Yes.' Then a four pounder. Finally the other chap has a bass – or something that will grow into a bass one day, a perfect twenty centimetre scale model. One more three pounder to my rod and we call it a day. Only when I take my tackle down do I realise that I haven't been fishing a three ounce lead like my fishing partner, mine's only two and a half. And I'm sure it was the extra half ounce that made the difference. My bait was fishing from dip to dip, his bait was fishing wherever it landed. Another mucked-up guiding job.

The end of November and I head up to a north coast storm beach around low water. The surf's on the light side so I walk the length of the strand, looking for more fizz. Now this beach is hard white sand, and normally the wave arranges it in a series of ridges running parallel with the shore. But as I'm tramping along I come on an area the size of a tennis court that's pitted with scour-holes. They're full of stuff, weed, crabs, shells, little fish, even a gigantic pair of tartan Y-fronts. I make a mental note of the spot so I can give it a few casts when the tide comes up and covers it. At half-tide I do just that. Three casts, three sandeels, three bass, topping out at five-and-a-quarter pounds. And I manage to avoid the Black Watch underpants as well.

- Two species always hook themselves securely: baby congers and weevers. And unlike a bass a lump of weed rarely comes off in the shallows. Murphy's Law strikes again.

- I love the shipping forecast. Dogger, Fisher, German Bight, Humber, Thames, Dover, Wight, Portland, Plymouth, Biscay. Even Bob Dylan never sounds that good, and he won a Nobel Prize.

- I spend a lot of fishing time polishing my glasses, wiping off fog, drizzle, and sea spray. I'm always reminded of an advertising slogan that used to be in *The Times* when I was a boy: 'You can't be optimistic with a misty optic.'

I'm convinced also that a moving bait's more attractive to bass than one that just sits on the bottom. I think a little motion must draw attention to my squid, fish, worms, or shellfish, like a flashing neon sign outside a snack-bar. A lot of my bites come almost as the lead's settling into its new spot. And on the rare occasions when I use two baits – usually in cold spring weather, when there's not a lot going on – I'll catch nothing for a long while, then a double-header. You might say this is because the fish are in shoals, but usually it's two different species, so I reckon it's down to movement. Once a codling or whiting has grabbed a bait, the other bait starts jigging about like a well-sloshed tourist at a ceilidh, and a foraging bass can't resist it.

Of course wandering tackle means you can't shove your rod onto a tripod and sit down for a Cornish cream tea, you have to keep it in your hand. Myself I don't own a tripod, but I find it hard even to use my sand-spike. When I was a youngster I fished with an older gentleman. If he saw me rest my rod or go too long without a fresh bait, he'd give a sad little smile and say, 'Fish like you mean it, or don't fish at all.' So when my fingers are numb from an east wind off the Russian steppes, when I think how good it would feel to shove the rod against the sand-spike and stick my hands in my pockets, I find I'd rather freeze and suffer than let down the old boy's memory. And holding the rod's a plus anyway. I think I convert more bites into hook-ups and avoid deep hook-holds by feeling every first twitch. What I know for certain is that a held rod means you don't need to keep your eyes glued to your rod-tip, you can use them to find fish.

Lure-nuts and fly-chuckers don't need to be persuaded of this. If they're any good they're scanning the briny all the time, looking for fins, swirls, jumping baitfish, terns or gannets hitting the water, cormorants duck-diving, and out-of-control kayak-racers. But the beach-fisher can pick up handy information as well, even in darkness. Where's the wave breaking, does that mean a new sandbar? Where's the water smooth, could that be a gully? In the half-light seals give you pointers on how far to cast. Obviously I'm not going to fish right where they're feeding, but they're dab hands at working out which wave holds the most prey species.

- 'Pensioner's monster,' was a headline. That's rude: he isn't just a pensioner, he's a bearded boat-fisher from Bude – who happens to be over sixty-five.

Late November, cold and still. Fishing conditions, in a word, were rubbish; in two words, total rubbish. But I had a few lugworms that wouldn't make it to another day, so away to a nearby beach over high water. Now this beach runs down in two shelves, one just below the high tide mark, the other just above low. Fish tend to concentrate right on the drop-offs, but there's no hard-and-fast rule as to which drop-off's going to do the trick. So a cast of forty-odd yards and I twitched the weight in until I could feel the steep slope of the shelving bottom. Not a sniff. Then a five yard flick to the closer shelf. Equally odourless. As the light came up I saw two seals feeding busily, then two more. They were all about twenty yards from the margin, on neither drop-off, smack in the middle of the flat area of the beach. I walked along the shingle for a few hundred yards and tried a twenty yard lob. Two schoolies and a codling in about ten minutes. I'm not too bad at chasing fish, but I'm not a patch on a seal. (Despite my furry face I'm not as cuddly-looking either.)

So with any sort of luck we now have a fair idea when, where, and how to find feeding bass. Not quite as important as finding them – though shopping-mad lure-maniacs obsess about it – comes the next decision, what should we offer by way of lure, fly, or bait? A good many fishers on my patch would tell you that's a non-issue. Plenty of West Cornish lure-jockeys swear by a sandeel shad, they use it day in and day out, varying only the size and the colour. Holiday folk often have favourites as well, usually expensive Japanese plugs like Gunfish, Feed-Shallow, Patchinko, Sammy. Fly-fishers love their Clouser Minnows and Bucktail Deceivers. And lots of the regulars on surf beaches would tell you, 'The answer's lug. What was the question?' But I don't agree, perhaps because of my trout-fishing years. For trout, matching the hatch is key. If the fish are on a green buzzer, you need to imitate a green buzzer. Put anything else on the water and you'll go swivel-eyed bonkers. Fish after fish will come up to your fly, then turn away at the last second, like a foodie eyeing up a chain-store nose-and-tail-burger. You can almost hear them sneering at you: 'A daddy-longlegs in a buzzer hatch, why would I be daft enough to eat that?'

Now I don't think bass are anything like as fussy as trout. When a trout's locked in on a hatch of buzzers, that's all it'll take, a fly with the right size, shape, colour, and movement in the water. And bass go for a much more varied diet. I eat quite a lot of bass, which means I do my share of gutting and filleting (always supervised by the cat who has the scraps). Sometimes I clean a fish with a stomach full of just one thing. But a good many bass have been enjoying the opportunist's tasting menu, a prawn starter, a crab main course, a sandeel for pudding. Still I believe they'll bite better if you spare them the trouble of switching from one prey species to another, just offer them something they're finding and eating anyway. And once in a while they home in completely onto a single food source. I see this most often with weed maggots, whitebait, and jelly-fry.

So when I fish lures or the fly I try to cast something that suggests the bait species that's in the water: sandeels, baby mullet, whitebait, little fry, prawns, whatever. Getting the size more-or-less right is very important. A whitebait-feeder often has a good look at a big plug, but that's all it has, a swirling, boiling, sanity-shredding look. To persuade it to hit I like something whitebait-sized, usually a small Toby. I don't think colour and finish matter as much as size and shape, but getting them right as well can only help the cause. That's why I'm such a fan of the silver and white Toby, to my eye it looks just like a dying whitebait when it's in the water.

July, an early morning lure-fishing session, I was planning to finish before the carpark lady arrived to ask for my three quid. But I wasn't so sure I'd be able to tear myself away from the rocks, there were bass swirls all over the shop and the tide line was spotted with dead sandeels. So I tried a slim shallow-diving plug. A couple of follows, no takes. Switch to a smaller version in a paler colour. Same story, swirls but no pulls. A twenty gramme Toby on a slow retrieve, then a fast one, and finally a hit. It wasn't a bass so much as a bassette, maybe half the size of a legal fish, but it was a lucky catch.

As I unhooked it, it spat out its last few snacks. It was like one of those magic tricks where a conjuror pulls ping-pong balls out of someone's mouth. Out came a one inch jelly-fry, then another, then another, then another. Question answered, the better bass weren't hitting my lures because they were feeding on tiddlers. So what did I have in my lure-box that was small enough? Nothing. Out with the fly-box. I tied a short dropper into a piece of monofilament, put a size six silver and white muddler on the dropper, the Toby on the point, and gave it a chuck. Bang, first cast, a half-decent bass. I squished the barb on the fly and I lost count of the fish I caught and released. Then a pair of holiday-makers pitched up. They'd been plugging away for two hours, not a single offer; and they looked as cheery as grid-locked commuters with indigestion. I only had one spare muddler minnow so the second visitor got a home-tied silvery effort. It made not a bit of difference. If the fly was about an inch long and more-or-less the right shape it was a winner.

When it comes to the surf I don't think using the right bait is quite so important. Put a chunky crab or two, a few lugworms, a whole squid close to feeding fish, and likely you'll see some interest. But it still makes sense to present something the bass might be targeting naturally, that can turn some interest into a non-stop orgy of bites. And I have a theory on this one. No scientific evidence to support it, just backside-of-the-trouser-waders intuition, but here goes. I reckon bass feed by sight if they can, only falling back on smell if the water's really cloudy.

For one thing their eyes are pretty enormous, well suited to hunting in low light. And we know they'll find and smash a lure – even one with no rattles and not much movement – when it's as dark as the bottom of a coal-sack. What's more, chasing them with soft artificials tells me they could take a Dulux shade-card and come up with a kitchen colour-scheme on a moonless night with thick cloud cover.

It was the end of April, usually time to get a bit serious about lure-fishing. The water was up to twelve or thirteen degrees and there was a gentle onshore breeze. I woke up way too early (as usual), but you can only waste so much time on a cup of coffee, so I took myself down to a rocky point in Mount's Bay. It was pitch dark and I didn't want to scare away the fish with my torch, so I clambered to the mark as the four-legged man (two feet, one hand, one bottom). My lure was clipped on already, a weedless and weightless soft plastic stick-bait in a dingy brown lugwormy colour. Flick it out, then don't do a thing, not a sausage, just let it sink. And it can't have been deeper than a couple of feet when it was clobbered by a school-bass. In half an hour I caught three small bass and missed three other pulls. Then I noticed that the lure wasn't casting too well, felt a bit light. I ran my fingers over it and found the tail end had been chewed off. I dug out a replacement and managed to clip it on as well, all without using my torch. Cast it out, let it sink, twitch it in. Twenty minutes of this routine, not so much as a nibble. As the first light came up I gave my lure a quick once-over. This one wasn't dingy brown, it was a wild electric blue, like a platform-shod glam-rocker's flared trousers. I swapped it for another brown one and I was back into the fish.

So bass seem to have sharp enough eyesight to hunt on visual even on the darkest night. But that doesn't mean they do it. After all, most of us have things we can do but don't bother with. I know from my wasted youth that I can drink a bottle of scotch without falling over, but I haven't tried it since the 1970s. So why would sight be the bass's default setting when it's on the food trail? And I suspect it's down to scope and efficiency. I've seen bass move to a fly – a size eight no less – from twenty feet away, and I'm not sure their sense of smell is as slick as that. With a twenty foot range, a sight-feeding fish can set herself up in a prime spot where she monitors a whole bunch of pots and depressions – the regional editor of the *Good Bass Pub Guide* – then swims over to whichever holds the most tasty things to eat. Minimal travel, lots of food – perfection.

And if bass do indeed rely on their eyes in clean water, their sense of smell in the mucky stuff, this helps us narrow down the baits we choose. For me a clear sea means an eye-grabber: a bunch of wriggling ragworms, a big shiny sandeel, or a frisky hard crab. A stir-up means juice: lugworm, whole squid, razor clam, mussel, or peeler. (I don't use peeler a lot. They're tedious to catch, expensive to buy, and I hardly ever find them in bass's stomachs except for a couple of weeks in late spring.) Dead mackerel swings both ways, a whole joey's a sight bait, a fillet or a head's a scent bait. And small live fish – whiting, pout, pollack, and so on – rely on sight and on the bass picking up their vibrations.

Easterly breezes, Mount's Bay was like a millpond. The water temperature was about nine degrees so I didn't rate my chances with lures. (Besides it was pretty chilly, and you can't lure-fish or fly-fish without both hands out in the weather, but you can hold a beach rod with one hand while you put the other in your pocket.) Anyway I had a few old lug so I decided on a couple of hours over low water. Every cast was the same, quick rattles and a stripped bait – whiting. I wandered along the sand, paddling through a shallow gully. In the middle of the dip I felt something tap my wader, a whiting about seven inches long. With skill that would have dumbfounded any Premier League striker – especially given that I'm a clumsy old chap with a limp – I flicked the tinker up the beach. I took off my weight, stuck a 6/0 through the whiting's back just aft of the middle, and tossed it into the shallows. Every time I tightened the line it tried to swim away, so pretty soon I had it twenty-odd yards out. Then came a huge thump followed by a run, a pause, then a longer run. It ought to have been a lunker, but no such luck, a two pound schoolie. (Using pollack as live-bait I once had a bass that was no longer than the pollack itself.)

- One advantage of fishing lures or the fly: your sandwiches don't taste of bait.

As well as adapting the bait to the clarity of the water I also try to match the hatch. By which I mean I prefer lugworm on a beach where I see lugworm casts, ragworm and mussel on white sand and mixed ground. Bits of mackerel are good near commercial and holiday fishing spots where heads and frames are tossed away. I like razor clam in places where I can hear their shells crunching as I walk. Whole squid and crab seem to work well when there's a big old surf running, plenty of edible flotsam in the wave; squid in coloured water, crab when it's clear. Sandeel serves me best at dawn and dusk, and on a sandy bottom.

Frozen squid, razor, mussel, and sandeel are cheap and very convenient to store. Fresh mackerel's a doddle, and hard crabs are easy to catch as well. Worm baits are a bit pricey if you buy them, free if you dig your own.

- To have lots of bites, go out with a dozen lugworm to use up. Murphy again.

Another thought on matching the hatch, why not make the bait look as natural as you can? I sometimes take a gander at the fishing magazines. They always seem to be showing us how to bait up with something or other, and it looks like high-tech surgery. Cut your peeler in half, take off the legs. Remove the quill from your squid. Snip the head and tail from a large sandeel. Why? Why would I dissect a peeler? Are bass looking for a neatly sliced crab? Or a boneless squid? Or a skilfully butchered sandeel? Do we think predators are like the judges on Masterchef: it tastes good, but your presentation isn't quite fine dining? I prefer to use everything the way a bass would find it in the wild.

With crabs I put the hook-point in one leg socket, out of another, and tie up with elastic. Squid goes on whole, one hook through the pointy end of the mantle, one through the open end and the head, and tie up again. Sandeel has the top hook through the tail end, the bottom hook through the head end (I've noticed that bass often eat them head first), and a bit more elastic thread. Lugworms go on tail first, and I leave a little tag when I tie on the hook, using it to stop the top worm slipping down the shank. Ragworms go on in a bunch of six or seven – so I prefer small ones, two or three inches long – with the hook nipped through about a quarter-inch of each worm's body, then out through its mouth. Razor clam, mussel, and mackerel fillet or head are two hook jobs, with elastic to make sure the points stay exposed.

And last of all, a proper bass bait's a big bait, a real mouthful. I see folk fishing with a single lugworm or ragworm artfully mounted on a tiddly hook – a size 2, even a 4. Not for me, I reckon a decent-sized bass would use up more than a lugworm's worth of calories swimming just half a yard to grab the wretched thing. A delicate little nibble's OK for an anorexic basslet, but I want chunky fish; and they prefer something more like a lorry-driver's fry-up, unlimited toast and tea. Four or five worms is as small as I ever go, even in schoolie season. And when there's a chance of a whopper I like an offering to fill the eye properly: two fat razor clams, a nine inch whole squid, a hard crab as big as a toddler's fist, a main-course sized bit of mackerel, and so on.

For five days in a row I caught bass between 64cm and 73cm every morning. I was fishing a beach that has lots of lugworm beds and where a good number of squid often wash up. So choosing a bait seems like a coin-toss. But I had a deeply-hooked fish on Friday and it came home even though it was only 48cm. I cleaned it and found bits of razor shell. All the good bass were on razor.

They say that information is power. I don't think that's right, but information can help you catch bass – as long as you keep thinking. The bait, lure, or fly that worked last time may or may not do the trick next time. And even when experience seems to give you clear direction, be prepared to ditch it and try something else. Never mind the right answer or the logical answer, just try to find an answer that works.

Bass need to survive – the idea

This is simple enough but fishers often ignore it. Bass need to fatten up, they also have an instinct for self-preservation, which keeps them away from dodgy situations. In big bass the instinct's well developed – otherwise they wouldn't have lived long enough to grow that big. Likely there a lot of things bass are programmed to avoid: seals, sharks (I've seen quite a few porbeagles at fishing spots), dolphins, being stranded, and who knows what. But from a fisher's point of view, three bass risk assessment factors loom largest.

First is thumps and splashes right in the middle of the fish's patch. Standing on a storm-lashed beach I've seen bass scarper when a dog bounded along the water's edge, so imagine what they do when it's a dirty great human body with size twelve boots bashing down the shore.

Second is light, especially if it moves or changes. One of my beaches is overlooked by a carpark. When someone pulls in and flashes high-beam lights onto the water, I'm fishing in the dead-and-buried sea for about twenty minutes.

Third is the human scarecrow. Again I've watched bass make high-speed tracks when a fisher stands outlined against the sky, flailing arms and gleaming rod sending wild semaphore alarm messages into the wave.

- You only catch fish when you fancy your fly or lure. Some people say confidence travels down the line. Nonsense, unless you believe in voodoo, ESP, UFO invasions, and fairies at the bottom of the garden. You just focus better when you think you're in with a decent chance.

Bass need to survive – how to fish

No quantum physics here, pretty obvious ideas, but I often see folk who catch fewer bass than they frighten away.

Waders are wonderful things. They keep your legs dry (mine cover my bottom as well). They let you walk out of spots where you've marooned yourself. You may need to wade to grab that fish-of-a-lifetime when she runs aground. So by all means wear waders. But I'd suggest you don't plosh out into the depths right away. Especially when it's calm I like to make my first casts standing well back from the water. When I've fished the margins, then it may make sense to wade through them – but not before. And remember you're on the shore, not an army parade ground, so step lightly in those big thumping boots.

Light's good stuff too. I know fishers who can tie Albright knots in the dark, but I'm not one of them. If I want to change my lure or fly, refresh my bait, pick fine weed from my line, I want a lamp. Most fishers like headlamps, often powerful, pricey ones. I don't. Too often I've seen someone with a headlamp turn it on, then hear an interesting sound behind. So now what happens? Whirl around to check out the noise, blast the water with umpteen hundred candlepower, and say goodbye to the next twenty minutes of fishing. I'm as absent-minded as anyone, so I use a five quid pocket torch, slim enough that it's comfortable between my teeth. When it's on it's in my mouth, and that's a constant reminder not to face the briny, even if I were to hear an ethereal voice saying, 'It's a miracle, the sea has turned into twenty-five year-old Islay whisky.'

And last of all, especially when it's flat, stay still and back from the water. You don't need to behave like some SAS-trained sniper, you just want to be a bit thoughtful. On rock marks I stand or sit somewhere that means I'm not backlit by the moon or the breaking dawn. On calm beaches I keep well away from the shoreline. Dull-coloured clothing may help too, an excuse for my disgraceful fishing togs – the mud, weed, and squid ink are camouflage. Jumping about in the shallows like an amphibious Morris dancer on the cider certainly sends the bass in the direction of the exits.

It was late July, a warm night with a gentle onshore breeze, a quarter-moon, and a small but lively wave. I started fishing mid-way through the ebb and it was a bite on almost every cast. They weren't any size – summer neaps often deliver a lot of schoolies – but it was great fun. After an hour another fisher showed up and asked me what was going on. Lugworms, twenty yards, loads of smallish bass. So he wandered off and made a cast. Now I like to fish sitting down – it's a long story, best summed up by a South African surgeon who X-rayed my legs and torso, peered despairingly at the plates, then told me, 'Man, you have an orthopaedic death-wish.' And on the ebb I sit back from the waterline, it just isn't worth chasing the tide as it drops. So I was propped on my little backpack-cum-stool maybe ten yards up the shore. The other fellow stood in the shallows, looking like a studiously posed publicity photo from the Irish tourist board. In the time we were together on the beach he had three bass and a missed bite, I had eleven. I might well be wrong, but I think his body was scaring the fish away from his bait.

- I was on a moonlit storm beach and the wave was huge, too rough for decent sport. Then I saw a torch coming towards me. It was a young couple from Wisconsin, on holiday, looking for their Cornish roots. Jet-lagged and sleepless, they were going for a walk. I suggested the dunes instead of the beach: it was dry one minute, a heaving maelstrom the next. So off they went, and in twenty minutes I saw the light again. But by now the young fellow was on the sand, running out behind the wave, hollering like an eejit, then haring back in front of the next one. Of course this didn't last, and he was hit by a wall of swell. Winded, concussed, or both, I could see a limp body in the shallow foam, face-down, drifting like a dead eel. So I grabbed my sand-spike and out into the surf. I collared the lad and dragged him half-way

Almost six pounds. Summer, and the sea was jumping with one inch jelly-fry. Bass would follow just about any lure in the box, but they wouldn't hit. For a week or so a small seatrout fly or a white muddler, size 6 or 8, was your only man, fished on regular fly gear or on a dropper ahead of a lure.

A lot of lure-fishers have go-to favourites, often expensive plugs. That's fine, but I reckon it's best always to imitate roughly what the bass are eating already. And sometimes you have to match the hatch precisely – especially when the fish are on easy-to-catch foods like weed maggots or very small fry. As a rule I like bigger baits for bigger bass, but every rule has its exception.

By the way the swimming pool behind me is at a friend's house. Apart from the shower I only ever go in the water up to my knees, and always in trouser-waders.

up the beach. Then another wave crashed in, pushing me up the shore and filling my waders. By now the young chap was conscious, so I sploshed and waddled up to my car – which is always full of tackle, spare clothes and suchlike – and offered to rustle up a towel and a dry fleece. But the woman said their B and B was very close by, so no need. Then they asked if they could pay me. 'Not at all,' I said, 'but if you want to, just put something in a charity collection box.'

I wrote up my little adventure on a forum site and forgot all about it. Then a while later someone sent me an email with a copy of a letter to his local paper in Wisconsin. It urged folk to visit Cornwall, it was lovely and the people were wonderful. Her fiancé had been saved from drowning by a local fellow. What's more this fellow had refused payment – even though he was a homeless fisherman living in an old Nissan Micra.

Now at the time my daughter had just started college, and one of her new friends liked to tease her because she'd been to a private school. 'Aren't we posh, Daddy probably drives a Jaguar.' Next time he said it, she was ready. 'No, not really. According to the newspaper he's a homeless fisherman living in an old Nissan Micra.'

• Fishers are among the most trustworthy people you meet. They tell so many lies about fish that got away that they have none left for everyday life.

• Don't you hate it when someone asks if you've had any luck? It isn't luck at all, it's consummate skill allied with zen-like focus and fanatical dedication. But I never say so.

CHAPTER FOUR

Choosing Fishing Spots

Bring me little water

As Bob Dylan put it (*Idiot Wind*, Columbia Records, 1975) '*I can't help it if I'm lucky*'. And I am. I live at the end of Cornwall, I can eat pasties without paying the prices they charge for exotic delicacies in main-line stations. What's more I'm a skip-and-jump from a coastline that faces north, south, or west, so in almost any weather I can find a mark where the wind direction isn't too bad. Also I've been self-employed for ages and sliding into retirement, which means fishing a few hours just about every day I'm home. That adds up to nearly two hundred trips a year, mostly in my favourite time-slot, from three hours before first light up until sunrise. By now you may be green with envy, and I apologise. But I paid my dues, a lot of years in Botswana, a wonderful place, but not for sea-fishing as it's land-locked; and a lot more in New York where I'd take a sixty minute subway ride to fish for small striped bass in a creek full of rusting Chevrolets.

- Half way through today's trip a true fisher is wondering where to go next time.

Anyway with all my outings you might wonder how many different spots I visit. Muck about on Google-Earth and count up the bass-lust inducing marks you can see on my patch. What say you, thirty, forty, a hundred? After all I fish lures, flies, and bait, so I need a variety of terrain.

But I have just seven regular haunts. Three are out-and-out storm beaches, two are rocky areas, one's an estuary, and one's a shingle beach. I believe it's better really to get to grips with a handful of spots than to have had a few chucks at a ton of places.

This isn't the way most fishers think. When folk have a chat in the tackle-shop they're always looking for marks they haven't tried before. Often all they find out is where to park and which bit of the shore's most popular; so they can show up in a crowd with no idea where the fish might be. That seems rather silly. And if someone catches a whopper and is daft enough to let on where it came from, that's a place that'll be visible from the space-station, newcomers streaming in from far and wide – even foreigners from as far and wide as Devon – and fifty-odd tip-lights brightening the night sky. And that has to be very silly indeed. The first-timers know nothing at all about this spot except that is has one less big bass than it used to – even if it was returned it's unlikely to stick around and be caught all over again.

Understanding a place properly takes time. You want to be able to find the bass-lies and the scoured out sandy patches even on the darkest night; and that means walking and fishing your marks at all states of the tide and in all sorts of wave and weather. I find the rotten days – flat calm, offshore gale – can be the ones that teach me most about my beaches and rocks. When fish are hard to come by, I do a lot more wandering and learning. And even when I have a spot pretty well figured out, my local knowledge needs to stay up-to-date. Most strands are unstable, a set of big tides can shift them around like Bob-the-Builder on amphetamines. So I'd say the bass fisher's best bet is to pick just a handful of areas, then focus bags of attention on them.

And how to pick them? Most people seem to go with the 'fifty other folk can't be far wrong' approach. A full carpark, enough headlamps to light a small city, acres of reports on websites or in tackle-shops, these are their signposts. Myself I'm not so sure. I'll pick any fisher's brain and I always seem to learn something, but I'd rather look for my own places to fish. Partly this is because I like to be by myself (that's the main reason I prefer early mornings to late evenings, less people around). Lights on the shore can put the bass right off, and crowded marks cut down my choices as to where to move and where to cast. But also I just like being alone, the only person daft enough to be standing in the wind and rain at three o'clock in the morning. Maybe I'm a sensitive, poetic soul or maybe I'm an antisocial bastard. Either way chasing bass is supposed to be a pleasure, so I'm looking for the spot less fished.

- I was chucking lures when I noticed a small seal on a patch of stones. He was trussed up with braid and he had a plug stuck in his head. I wondered if I could cut him free, but there was a bigger seal about five yards away. OK, I thought, forget about rescuing the little fellow, his mother will go crazy. Now I don't own a mobile telephone – I think they're the curse of our age – so I decided to go home and call the Seal Sanctuary. But as I walked up the shore, the big seal blocked my path. I veered left, she shuffled across to cut me off again. So perhaps she wanted me to take care of the nipper. Watching her out of the corner of my eye I walked up to the pup and started snipping with my knife. As I cut the last strand, he flicked his head and the lure flew through the air and planted itself in my chin. So I left the cove bleeding profusely and carrying a Japanese plug. For a couple of years those two seals would sit near me on the rocks and watch me fish, and they never stole anything from my line either.

A couple of afterthoughts. First, I found out that seal bites are very infectious, and that only one antibiotic prevents gangrene. Second, I identified my new plug from a tackle website. It was a twenty-five quid job, but all it ever seemed to catch was pollack – and seals and chins.

Another reason I don't follow the crowd is that popular marks often have water a lot deeper than I like. Fisher-folk are drawn to points with drop-offs and to shelving beaches. And for bass I'm looking for the opposite: shallow, weedy, fizzy water for the lures and flies, and flattish sand for the bait. Steep beaches often have one dumping breaker, but in a decent wave a gently dropping sea floor produces lots of white water and wave-tow; and that means a bigger treat-filled area for a foraging bass or three. By the same token, shallow water over a rocky bottom leads to plenty of swirls and eddies which stir up and discombobulate the prey species, while the lack of depth makes for easy hunting, nowhere for the tiddlers to hide away or escape. And so that's how I choose my spots. For lures and the fly I like a place where you'd take one look, then say, 'I'm not going to cast anything expensive into that tackle graveyard.' I want lumps, bumps, boulders, clumps of wrack, and hardly enough water to cover these plug-grabbing and fly-snagging features. A swipe of current – at least in the middle of the tide – is another feature of a desirable residence for feeding fish, lots of little rips to push their prey along and concentrate it. Easy access, a priority for a lot of folk, is a negative in my reckoning – when you need to crawl to your mark through muddy brambles it's less likely to have been hammered by other fishers. (Besides Murphy's Law tells us that convenient marks tend to be lousy marks.) A great way to find promising areas is by walking along cliff paths when it's too still and sunny for the fishing to be much good. (That's the oldie approach. Younger, more techie types go on virtual cliff-walks on their mobile telephones. I have callouses on my feet, they must have corns on their thumbs.)

October, time for the sea-spinach to sprout new leaves, and still blackberry season as well, so I went for a wander along the coastal footpath. I soon came across a double-header, clumps of new spinach and a thicket of berries as well, so I got busy. When the spinach bag was full I stopped for a ciggie and a stare at the water. I was looking over a small inlet popular with the day-time fly-fishers. It's shallow with a clean bottom, straightforward wading, and I'd never had a good bass from it. (Murphy's Law's very clear on this: comfortable underfoot conditions mean wee nippers.) But it had changed over the summer, loads of new weed. The mouth of the bay was choked with the stuff, just a six foot channel opening to the sea. Next morning I was down there for the last hour of the drop, a shallow-diver on my lure-clip. I waded gingerly across the bay, then I was at the channel. And sure enough the ebb was rushing out, boils and eddies like a river in full spate. I cast my lure into the middle of the current and let it wash to the edge of the stiller water. A slow turn of the reel and I was into a chunky bass. I had three that morning. But autumn's the season of mists, mellow fruitfulness, and monster gales; and a few days later all the weed was ripped away in a storm.

For bait-fishing I want a spot where a half-decent wave gives you lots and lots of sets of breakers, not just one big dump. Deep-water beaches are good for rum-runners and belly-flopping divers, but you can give me a strand that's flat or very gently sloping. If a twenty yard cast will put my gear into twelve or eighteen inches of water, that says we're on my kind of surf-beach. The only time I like a steep shore-line is in a calm. Then I'll fish flies, lures, or bait, but focus my attention on the area that's really close in, two to ten yards from shore, and all along the shelves and drop-offs.

Given a choice I'd go for a long beach or rocky section. Some fishers hate long beaches, you don't know where to start. I love long beaches. They take a while to learn, but they give you so many more options. You can move if the fishing's slow, if the weed comes in, if you're losing your wave. I also move if other people pitch up, especially if they settle in beside me and blast the surf with headlamps; or if they're noisy. Light on the wave kills the fishing, and noise makes me as happy as a Thatcherite Tory on a picket-line.

December, freezing cold and almost windless. The surf was dying and sport was as slow as a work-to-rule snail with lumbago. I scaled down to a one ounce lead to try to put a bit of movement into my bunch of ragworms, but they were just sitting on the bottom in splendid isolation, not even a weeny whiting or a woeful weever for company. Out of boredom I slung my rucksack on my back and went for a wander. After a mile I saw an enormous raft of weed in the shallows. Ankle-deep I walked up to it, there were little splashes everywhere. The weed was jumping with tiny fish, sand-hoppers, prawns, and crablets. So I took my lead off, added a few head-hooked ragworms to an

already jammed hook, and tossed my bait twenty feet out, just to the side of the weed-mat. A little twitch and I was into a three pounder. Nothing to do the clod-hopping wader dance about, but it's always fun to catch a bass in rotten conditions.

Another thing, if I'm going to fish a new spot, or somewhere I haven't been for a while, I do it on an ebbing tide. On the flow it's easy to set up, then be surprised by the rising water level and a big wave. And in my neck of the woods the regular surf is often compounded by enormous and omnivorous swells from the mid-Atlantic. I've met plenty of fishers searching for rods, tripods, lure bags and suchlike that have been sucked away into the briny. And they were the lucky ones. Every year folk are washed out to sea, and their flotation suits just make it easier to find their corpses. Myself either I'm very prudent or I'm a devout coward – and I reckon they're one and the same thing. An old Cornish lobsterman I knew in my youth had it right: 'Of course I'm not afraid of the sea, my handsome. I'm not ignorant and I'm not stupid. So I'm effing terrified of it.'

• As a boy I spent hours on the rocks with a net. I'd bring my catch home, we'd boil the shrimps up in seawater, then peel them at the table. People hardly seem to bother these days, they think of a shrimp or a prawn as some giant creature from a pond in Thailand, so the little chaps in the tidal pools don't measure up. I used to hunt field mushrooms as well, but very few folk do that nowadays, too many health-and-safety wonks chuntering about toxic fungi. My other hobby was collecting empty soft drink bottles which you could take to the grocer's shop at threepence a whack. We didn't have foraging workshops or a recycling movement in my childhood, just a bit of common-sense.

When I was a junior the commercial boatmen used to talk about the May Gales, this was one of them, screaming in from the south-west with gusts up to fifty miles per hour. I took

a packet of big unwashed squid down to a Mount's Bay beach,
where one look at the surf told me all I needed to know: a ten
foot dump, weed like King-Kong's failed macramé project. But
this beach is about three miles long, I wondered if it might be
fishable at the east end. It was a long enough walk – the closest
parking spot's about a mile short of the east-most point – and it
felt even longer in the wind and the stinging rain. But the further
I tramped the smaller the wave and the less frequent the clumps
of weed. I wound up fishing in a six foot surf for a ray, a dogfish,
and two bass, both just over three pounds.

- Dog-walkers often ask why I don't become a commercial rod-and-line bass fisher. No chance. When a good fish sheds the hook, the air turns somewhat blue. Imagine what would happen if I'd just lost fifty quid as well. Indigo.

A last thought – and this isn't always possible – but I love spots that are covered by nearby surf prediction sites. I can check the wind by looking out of my windows at home, watching the turbines. But a breeze is only one of the things that create an inshore wave – along with tide, barometric pressure, incoming swell, recent ocean storms, and who knows what else. Now I'm a bit of a sceptic when it comes to forecasters. Maybe a complete sceptic. Whether they tell us about the weather, the surf, the economy, or who's going to win the last race at Market Rasen, I reckon they spout a lot of appalling drivel. But most of the surfie websites, along with all the maps and tables, have live cameras. What they say about the future may be science-fiction, and a lot more fiction than science as far as I can tell; but the web-cam doesn't lie, so at least I can have an idea about today's sea-state as I plan tomorrow's outing.

It was early December and the weather chart was a beauty,
south-west wind, force five, backing west-south-west. Warmish
as well, and no more than a few spots of drizzle. So at about five-
thirty in the morning I took myself and a bag of big unwashed

squid down to a beach that faces south-west, expecting to be greeted by a few sets of lively breakers. Fat chance. I know their motives aren't the same, but the weather-people seem to talk almost as much tripe as politicians. The wind was howling out of the north-north-west, the sea was flat but with what surfers call a dumpy wave, and I clambered out of the car into a frigid horizontal downpour so typical of the English Riviera. I walked down to the water's edge and had a ponder. Rotten wave, where might it be better? North in the wind does a quick job on the surf on this particular beach, flattening it out like a Formula One trouser-press. I shut my eyes and tried to imagine the place in daylight, and there was at least a bit of an idea. There's a big sandy ridge towards the east end of the bay, that might keep some wave. So I shouldered my bag and hiked a mile into the distance, chilly dribbles trickling down my spine. And it worked. It wasn't terrific bass-fishing surf, but it wasn't completely dead. Two bass and a baby ray, and I know jolly well I wouldn't have caught them without my soggy little route-march.

Mid-June, I took my lure-rod to a little run of coves. From a distance the wave looked as good as the forecast, a decent froth on the surface. Then I arrived at the first cove, there wasn't any blasted surface, just an unbroken mat of wrack; and I've never found a website that predicts infestations of seaweed. I looked at the wave. Messiah for a day, I thought, I can walk on the water. But the tide was pulling right to left, and that gave rise to a thought: this solid twenty yard clump of shite might at least act as a kind of dam, stopping any other bits of weed from reaching the down-tide side. So I scrambled back onto the cliff, hiked half a mile, and slither-bumped down to the next access point. Not a scrap of weed to be seen. (As it turned out the fishing was rubbish – just a school-bass – but it was a lot better than not fishing at all.)

SONG OF THE SOLITARY BASS FISHER

- I was fishing a rising surf on Boxing Day and I had a few small bass and one decent fish. At dawn the surfers started to arrive. As usual most of them were as good as gold: clock a fisher, move along the sand, and stay sensibly far away from my gear. But then a pair of dipsticks showed up. Not local, they sounded like old-Etonians, that curious bray that reminds me of a suffering donkey. Anyway one of them proceeded to surf straight across my line. I yelled a suggestion – anatomically improbable at best – and moved quarter of a mile upwind. And the half-wits followed me and ran over my gear again – twice. So I waited until they came out of the water. Then I asked with polite curiosity whether they were stupid or just so far up their own backsides as to not even notice me fishing. 'Oh, we didn't know you were fishing,' drawled one. 'I understand,' I told him, 'an easy mistake to make. I might be trying to commit slow suicide, standing by the water, holding a carbon fibre fishing rod, and waiting for a lightning storm.' It's a rare delight when you think of the right thing to say before it's too late to say it.

- One of those days when you wonder if you'll have enough bait, two bass on my first two casts. Then I saw a fellow with three rods. A grunt, a mighty fling, and his weight must have landed in the Scillies – but not among the bass. I advised him to try closer in, but no sale, he knew his stuff, he'd been fishing for fifteen years. 'OK,' I thought, 'You can lead a horse to water, but rhubarb must be forced.' So I wandered on. When I headed back, there was the stranger, one of his beach-casters thumping wildly. 'It's a monster,' he yelped, 'Could you run to my car for the gaff?' My first thought: 'I'm sixty-odd years old, I walk with a limp, and you want me to run to your car?' But I scurried off. 'Would you wade in and get it.' I headed into the surf, listening to a commentary and wondering whether I too should try casting half-way across the ocean. 'It's running in. A head-shake, but I can see the leader.' And there it was, a five gallon plastic bucket bouncing around in the wave.

A proper big fish wave in Mount's Bay. The last breaking wave was about 100 yards from the shore, the feeding fish were 25 to 30 yards out. Coloured surf's almost inevitable in a sea like this, so generally I use big unwashed squid. And a wired lead's the only way to keep the bait in the water.

There's a rocky outcrop at the west end of the beach. It can be good for lures and the fly, but not in these conditions. Up-country may be different, but add a full-blown Atlantic swell to an inshore wave and you have a nasty accident waiting to happen. I sometimes see fishers on promontories in horribly rough weather. I imagine they think they're rugged and determined. Selfish eejits more like, expecting volunteers from the RNLI to put themselves in harm's way when something predictably goes wrong.

Sunrise in Mount's Bay, almost time to head home for a coffee. In winter I fish until it's fully light, but generally I like the last hours of darkness and the first glow of dawn.

Except around high water this south-facing beach is pretty flat. This seems to help it to hold some sort of a wave even in settled weather. Three or four sets of building breakers, and I was casting ragworms between the biggest wave and the next one in, maybe 25 yards. Four bass, the best about six pounds. Another fisher was hurling his bait 80-odd yards. I tried to get him to fish closer in, but he was having none of it. He caught one whiting as big as his thumb. When you can see another chap catching bass in the shallows, why on earth wouldn't you have a try at least? Jim Morrison was on the money, 'People are strange' (The Doors, Elektra Records, 1967).

Good-looking lure-fishing terrain seen from the cliff path. Good for the fly as well. Shallow, rocky, weedy, and a swipe of tide – just what I like. Of course I took the snap on a calm day in bright sunshine. But before dawn, with a breeze to fizz things up, we'd be talking. Often the best fishing's within a few feet of the water's edge.

If it looks like a tackle graveyard, that's because it is. On low springs I re-fill my lure box from the shallows, picking up plugs that are out of my price range. I'd never spend twenty-five quid on a lure, but I'll use a free sample.

My rough guide to fishing with artificials: if you're not worried about snags you're in the wrong spot. Lumps and bumps and clumps concentrate the prey species – and the feeding bass. And shallow water helps them hunt with minimal effort.

CHAPTER FIVE

Gear for the Bass Fisher

I don't need no diamond ring, don't need no Cadillac car

If you read the angling press or browse a few forums you can wind up thinking you'd catch more bass if you bought a spiffier rod, a three hundred quid surf reel, or a stupendous new lure, priced as if carved by Michelangelo and painted by Rubens. No surprise, magazines make money from advertising and the forums seem to be stuffed with tackle-junkies; so nobody's going to tell you what I reckon, which is that a lot of kit's unnecessary or unhelpful. With a couple of exceptions I don't think snazzy tackle makes anyone more successful with the bass. Of course I don't mean you should chuck your precision-built multiplier in the recycle bin or replace your posh plugs with cheap imitations. Some fishers enjoy using nifty gear just as some folk enjoy driving a fancy car. But a new BMW in the carpark won't get you any extra bites, and nor will a top-of-the-line rod or reel. Somewhere I read a little prayer: 'If I die, please don't let my family sell my tackle for what I said I paid for it.' No such worries here, I'm frugal to the point of squeakiness. But it works for me.

And first off there are two purchases that at least sometimes make bass fishers less successful, the tripod and the headlamp. I'm sure tripods are great for some sorts of fishing, but for bass they're about as much use as a three piece suit on a nudist beach. Dump the tripod, dump the tip-light, and hold the rod. This lets you fish a light sinker so your gear can wander around in the wave, finding the gullies and depressions. That'll lead to a lot more takes than anchoring your bait to the bottom with a walloping great wired lead. I also think it's easier to turn offers into hook-ups when the rod's in your hand – a big bass often takes as gently as a baby flounder that thinks it might be lugworm-intolerant. I reckon a held rod leads to less swallowed baits as well, swifter releases. And I know for sure that folk with tripods don't move – to find a better wave, to look for fish, to avoid weed – as much as the fisher with less hardware. Once they've set up their base camp they act like Brits on comfy pool-side loungers in Spain, they stay put.

Headlamps aren't always a handicap, but I often see them used as an expensive bass-repellent. Fishers with good light discipline do fine with headlamps. Ordinary mortals forget there's a searchlight stuck to their noggins and turn to look at the water. Some even use their lamps to wade in and cast. And once you've beamed your LEDs all over the waves you can sing Camborne Hill for the next twenty minutes, you're not going to do any good on the fishing front. Bass come inshore for an easy feed not a boogie at the disco, so a flashing light show's a big turn-off. I like a pocket torch. I hold it in my teeth, then switch it off before I face the water.

Now a couple of things that won't do any harm but won't help either, unless you're a total gadget-head: shock-leaders and bait-clips. I see people using them, but they're a waste of time and money. For bass you'll never have to cast hard enough or far enough to need them. Also the knot that joins a shock-leader to the main-line is a magnet for little bits of weed, and any knot's a possible weak spot in your set-up.

- Three ways to tell someone's a real bass fisher:
  1. Lots of spikey gashes on the hands – trebles, fins, and gill plates are devils.
  2. Yellow-stained fingers – lugworm juice never really comes off.
  3. Bass-fishing cologne, Eau de Calamari, can't miss it.

OK, those are two things not to take on a bass trip and two more that just fritter away your hard-earned cash. Now for the please-yourself bits of kit, the rod and the reel. For lure-fishing any rod that casts a sensible weight (I like ten to thirty-ish grammes) will be fine. Some folk favour tiny little short rods, some – like myself – prefer something more like an old-fashioned salmon spinner, ten or eleven feet long. But anything that'll chuck a lure into the right spot is going to catch its share of bass. The mini-rods may be better for pure lure-fishing, and if they're red and Japanese they win you admiring stares from the people who pore endlessly over tackle-pornography websites. But longer, more traditional rods give you more choices. You can fish plugs, spoons, shads, and soft plastics; and you also can put on a float, a light leger rig, or a free-lined live-bait. Lure-fishing reels are a simple story. Decent line-lay and a smooth drag, that's all you need. If you can afford a top-of-the-line number and it gives you pleasure to use it, go for it. I buy spinning reels in the fifty-odd quid range. I don't need a life-time guarantee, my reels never wear out, they die violent deaths when their clumsy owner goes base over apex on some slimy bit of seaweed.

For fishing in the surf I'd say the rod should cast from two to four ounces. Some people like longer rods, some shorter, makes not a scrap of difference to the fish. Your rod has to feel comfortable in your hand, otherwise you'll be tempted to rest it – and that makes you into a bone-useless bass fisher. I use an eleven and a half footer and I honestly prefer cheap, soft-actioned rods. My back-up's a flash job which I bought for twenty quid from a red-faced chap who was going to chuck it in the sea because the effing French had killed all the bass so what was the effing point any-effing-way.

I slipped my fish bag discreetly into the car boot and made him an offer. His rod was new, a hundred and thirty pounds in the on-line shops. It casts amazingly well even with just a flick. Probably too well, making it easy to fish too far out, so I don't like it half as much as the floppier ones that list for twenty-odd quid. Surf reels, anything that'll hold enough line to give you confidence, as long as it has winching power – pumping bass through the shallows is a good way to shake them off, I reckon. I prefer a fixed-spool, but your choice. You're not going to be doing any distance casting anyway, not for bass, so don't worry, be happy.

• A lot of people hurl their gear miles out and fish in the deepest water they can reach. I blame the cinema. Film monsters always come out of the abyss, we've been conditioned to think that's where they'll be lurking. Wrong. I hope I'm not spoiling anyone's fun, but that shark in *Jaws* was a mechanical model.

Fly-fishing gear can set you back an arm and a couple of legs, and if you want to hurl big streamers into a gale I'm sure you need some pretty clever kit – and a lot more casting skill than I'll ever have. But I tend to take my fly-rod to calm coves and small shallow sea-pools, so I just use an old trout outfit with a number seven weight-forward floating line. Other fishers tell me it's not beefy enough for bass, but it's taken a seven pounder. It's a good idea to have lots of backing, but the reel can be cheap and simple, it's only a place to keep your line. Tapered leaders strike me as a waste of money, and specialised bass flies can be daylight robbery. I saw Clouser Minnows for four quid each the other day, and even a fumble-fingered chap like myself can tie up a half-decent imitation of a sandeel or a whitebait. If you don't make flies, I'd say you're better off buying seatrout or salmon patterns than paying silly money for the trendy stuff. As long as the size and shape more or less match what the bass are eating, I find the precise tying makes no real difference.

Right, so now I've given up any chance of being sponsored by rod and reel companies or fly-tyers. No worries, I'm not spending much anyway. But there are a couple of tackle items where I fork out a bit, and the first is braid. I was a late convert to braid, even on my lure outfit. After fifty-odd years I was a crusty traditionalist, dyed-in-the-monofilament. Then I won a spool of four-strand and I was too thrifty not to give it a go. And now I'm the universal braid-man. I use it on my lure outfit and on my beach reel as well. With lures it makes casting so easy, even when I use a tiny weightless soft plastic. It also lets me pull my gear out of snags – the hook often straightens before the braid pops.

People say it helps with the detection of takes as well, but I never have a problem picking up a hit. Bass can attack soft lures tentatively, like nervous diners sampling incendiary curries, but they're not mullet, subtlety's not their style.

- I've been told wrasse is good eating. You wrap fillets in bacon, then fry them with garlic. I'm not sold. Cooked like that my waders would be tasty.

On the beach I find my braid even more helpful. Not for casting, because I could cast to typical bass range with kitchen string. No, I like braid in the surf because I fish in all sorts of gnarly sea-states and weathers. A howling cross-shore gale, mono makes a parachute along the beach, braid stays tighter to the terminal tackle. A massive sucking sea, same story, the thinner diameter of the braid means less drag, so I can use a lighter weight. And braid doesn't stretch, which helps me stay in close touch with my gear as it hops and skips along the bottom. Last of all, because it's so thin I use thirty pound braid on the beach. I make most of my rigs from twenty-five pound mono, so a snag-up usually means I break off the weight or the hook, nothing more.

- Why do dogfish always look as if they're smiling? Do they know something we don't know?

It was one of those summer spells when most of the holiday-makers look miserable, cowering behind their stripy beach shelters like upland sheep in a blizzard. The only folk smiling are the bass fishers, the kite-surfers, and the hot pasty sellers when there's a thirty-five mile per hour wind whipping across the shore. I fished a four ounce bomb and it was almost holding, just bouncing a few feet from time to time. I managed three decent bass and a few babies. Back at the car I ran into another fisher. He was cheery as well, two chunky bass to his rod. And of course we had to compare notes. He was on lug, I was on squid. He was using an eight ounce breakaway, and how on earth had I been using a bomb? His main-line was twenty pound mono, the wind had been dragging his gear along the shore.

And now the second area where I'll pay for quality: hooks (and no thought of free kit for endorsements here – everyone has a price but even I'm not that cheap). Different folk go for different patterns – I like baitholders and Aberdeens – and leopards shouldn't change their spots. If you're a Limerick nut or a semicircle fan, be my guest.

The only thing about hooks I'd say with authority is that they need to be big and very sharp. I run between sizes 3/0 and 6/0 depending on the bait. Large hooks make it hard to catch tiddlers. Fine by me: they're rarely swallowed, they're good for monster or bass-sized baits, and they let you play a hefty fish with confidence – well, you may be shaking like a jelly when that whopper takes off, but you'd be even more blancmange-like if you were relying on a fine-wire size 4. And razor sharp points are a no-brainer. When I buy new hooks I test each one. A tenth of them go straight in the bin. And on the shore it's muscle memory: change the bait, check the point. If it's not still vicious, sharpen it or replace it.

Hooks on lures are just as vital and often ignored. I meet holiday fishers with flash rods, high-end reels, designer bum-bags, film star sunglasses, twenty quid plugs, and rusty trebles that wouldn't penetrate the skin of a damp rice pudding. Now I don't recommend changing lure-hooks out there on the rocks. For that chore I sit at my desk with my pliers, my knife, and a wodge of paper towel, and the process always involves a lot of bloodshed and blasphemy. But on the fishing mark you can at least keep the points in decent nick with a stone or a miniature file; and if a hook's really banjaxed, switch to another lure.

Lures at dawn – which sounds like a costume drama with duelling anglers, frock coats and waders – the schoolies were as thick as thieves. Then a holiday fisher came along fishing a popper. It was fun to watch the bass charge at his plug and toss it in the air, but nothing was taking hold. The fisher was losing his mind, his commentary was as blue as a swimsuit model in a blizzard. The fellow sat down beside me and I ran my thumb over his hooks. They wouldn't have pierced a rotten apple. With all the politeness I could muster I suggested a different lure; and I left a happy chappie, catching and releasing bass to his heart's content.

- I was in the carpark when another car pulled in. Two fellows, one looked like a rugby player (about six-foot-six, lots of muscles), the other like a rugby ball (about five-foot-nothing, lots of tum and bum). As they sorted out their gear Mr. Rugby kept going on about how Mr. Ball should get himself a new rod, a seventeen footer. Now I've wondered about a long rod, so after a while I asked Mr. Rugby, 'What makes you think he needs a seventeen footer?' 'The weather,' said Mr. Rugby. That confused me, it was a warm, calm morning. 'What about the weather?' Mr. Rugby smiled: 'It feels like thunder, and I'm dead scared of electrical storms. But if I had George beside me holding a seventeen foot lightning conductor, then I'd feel safe as can be.'

- Good trout-fishers generally know about the life-cycles of the insects on their lakes and rivers, and some are decent entomologists. They try to imitate the fly that's on the water. A lot of bass fishers just sling out lugworms, a Sammy, or a Deceiver regardless of the season or the spot they're fishing. In the words of The Clash, it's food for thought (*Revolution Rock*, Epic Records, 1979).

A flying condom and a 20g silver and white Toby. Old-fashioned perhaps, but cheap and effective. The flying condom – basically a Mepps spinner with a latex tube body – catches bass, seatrout, salmon, flounder, golden-grey mullet, thick-lip mullet (on the drop) and pretty much anything else that swims. Fished quite slowly it's good for prospecting – when you don't know what kind of baitfish are in the water. I like the red body, but black would be my favourite. The Toby's a winner when the whitebait are in; and cranked really fast it's saved a lot of blank days. Even bass that aren't feeding often will have a go at something small and speedy.

There's nothing wrong with pricey lures, but tightwads like myself hesitate to cast them into the snaggy spots where big bass feed. And I'd rather fish something cheap in a good spot than something wonderful in a fish-desert.

- The brambles on the coastal footpath shred my trouser waders in short order, so I buy cheap ones. For a bit more money you can have waders to suit your body shape: RB for regular build, or FB which stands for full-bodied or fat bastard, depending who you ask. Unfortunately no one caters for us SBs (scrawny buzzards), so I do the belt up and plodge around with loose fabric flapping at my midriff. But guess what, you can buy waders made-to-measure, like Savile Row suits. I learned this from a lovely holiday-fisher I met in a cove. He saw me emptying leaves and twigs from my waist-band and showed me how his stocking-foot chesties were a perfect fit. I thought he might be embarrassed if I asked how much they cost so I looked it up on the internet. Starting around nine hundred quid, without the boots. I'm sticking with the cheap ones.

I sometimes use fancy lures – though many are from foraging trips at low tide.

IMA Salt Skimmer is great in water that's not as fizzy as I like. It's a surface lure, but not too splashy. It serves me best when there are small sandeels in the wave.

Megabass Dot Crawler is my favourite soft plastic. It doesn't need a weight, bass love it – even though it looks like a bit of seaweed or a thin turd – and softies are cheap, so I'm happy to use them through the snags. I fish it on a 5/0. The mucky colour of this lure is called Ayu, and I think it must suggest an overweight lugworm.

Maria Angel Kiss is a no-nonsense shallow-diver. I always take off the middle hook – who needs three trebles? It's good when baby mackerel or big sandeels are around.

And speaking of lures (here goes another sponsorship opportunity) I don't think the big money jobs are worth it. The things that make a difference, in order of importance, are putting the lure in the right place at the right time, moving it sensibly, and roughly what it looks like. Even when it comes to appearance I think size and shape are the pasty, everything else is the salad garnish they put on the plate so they can charge you an extra quid for your lunch. Match the hatch. If the length and outline of your offering look like a slow, crippled version of something the bass are chasing, most of the battle's won, whatever the colour scheme, the finish, or the minute details of the way it wobbles and wiggles.

I have old plugs that really do the job even though it's hard to tell what they looked like when they were new. Certainly they weren't designed to be gungy grey with white scratches, but the fish still love them – bass see colour, but nobody seems to know exactly how. Anyway most of my hard plugs are top-water jobs and shallow divers; and I'm quite sure the fish can't tell what the back of a lure looks like when they can only see its belly against the backdrop of the sky. So I'm happy with anything fishy-looking: silvery blue or green, pale and translucent, black and white, khaki-gold, and so on. I just avoid the really weird paint jobs, the ones like Grateful Dead tie-dye tee-shirts or lurid ice-lollies.

- Arriving on a beach I ran into the most delightful fellow who was heading home. He gave me his leftover bait, a few tired ragworms and one gigantic razor clam. First cast with the razor, almost as it landed, I had a gilthead bream of about four pounds. I felt I ought to head off after the other chap and give him his fish, but he was thirty years younger than me, he had a two hundred yard start, and I was in waders. That's my story and I'm sticking to it.

So what do you need in a sensible lure-box? A lot of folk on the forum sites seem to have a single favourite plug, a default choice, often Japanese and pricey. Fair enough, but I find the best lure to use depends on what the fish are eating right now. That says you want a few gizmos – hard plugs, shads, soft plastics, spoons, flies – to suggest the profiles of all the bass treats that show up on your patch. For me that means big sandeels, small sandeels, whitebait (a wee Toby), jelly-fry (a seatrout fly or a baby muddler minnow), weed-maggots (a pale grub-shaped fly), prawns (a palmer-dressed fly), worms (a weightless soft plastic with a lugwormy or ragwormy look), finger mullet, little pollack, and joey mackerel. Costly or cheap, I don't much care. In fact I reckon the cheap ones sometimes serve me better because I'm more willing to toss them into the lairy places – rocks, weed, sucking waves – where the bigger bass hold.

Some flies that have saved blanks when the fry or prawns are in. I'm bad at tying, but I reckon size and profile are what matter. The bottom right fly suggests a prawn – and it catches fish. Rough and ready, but the bass don't care.

High summer, oddly warm, and Mount's Bay's wall-to-wall with whitebait. Rumour has it that the landlord of one of our locals has been taking orders for them, then toddling off with a shrimping net and coming back to empty it into the fryer behind the bar. I arrive in the cove about an hour before dawn, the shore's ablaze with glowing eyes in the moonlight, twenty-odd foxes picking up whitebait that have been stranded by the tide. Until first light I fish a tiny little shallow-diving plug, one

I used to use for seatrout, maybe one-and-a-half inches long. It's so light that I can only cast it about fifteen yards, but it does the job, three schoolies up to a couple of pounds. Then at dawn I switch to a small silver and white single-hook Toby and catch a few more. On the way back to the cliff path I meet a holiday fisher, a fellow whose plugging outfit likely cost a bit more than my car. He's had nothing. 'They're going on whitebait,' I tell him, 'about two inches long.' He shows me his lure-box. Feed-Shallow, Patchinko, Sammy, Gunfish, nothing cheap, nothing under about four inches. 'I went out with a guide,' he says, 'he told me these were the best lures around here.' I'm thinking the guide likely sold him the plugs as well, about a dozen of them, twenty-odd quid each, a decent little side-line. 'I'm sure they're super lures, but not when the bass are on whitebait. Here, try a Toby, I've got a couple of spares.' I sit on a rock and roll a ciggie while he clips it on. And first cast he's into a chubby little bass about two pounds. 'Wow,' he says, 'that's a fantastic lure. What did you say it was called? And can I pay you for it? Or do you a swap for one of my plugs?' When I tell him I buy my Tobys in bulk, two quid apiece, he almost refuses to believe it.

And cheap or fancy there's an easy way of making hard lures and spoons last longer: a few thin coats of clear nail varnish. I buy so much that the lady in Boots must reckon I'm sniffing it. Hard-as-Nails is the best I've found. It's pricey for a nail varnish, but it means a lot less costly trips to the tackle-shop. If you tie flies it's great for finishing off the heads as well, and cheaper than the stuff in the fly-tying catalogues.

- Holiday folk sometimes ask me for advice on charter-boats. As a resolute fishing landlubber I'm inclined to be brief: 'Avoid the flaming things at all costs.' But if they demand my two-penny-worth, I default to logical analysis. First, find a captain with decent local word-of-mouth. A national reputation can come from good public relations as much as good fishing: bring a writer to your home port, provide a luxurious billet, tasty meals, and the finest wines available to humanity, and you can almost bank on a decent review even if the sport was rubbish. But local fishers just want big local fish and plenty of them.

Second, go with the no-frills option. If a boat prides itself on freshly made langoustine sandwiches, skinny lattes, and a luxury loo, that means the crew's too busy playing maître d'hôtel to do anything useful. If it offers a cold-box, some slush ice, and a wee over the transom, it's run by serious fish people. And third, other things being equal, go with the most weather-blasted skipper on the dock. The sea's a demanding work-place, it's only the canny mariners who stick around long enough to have wrinkles in their wrinkles.

A few more things come with me on every trip. Trouser-waders for one, I won't leave home without them. I don't go into the water much – wading's a mug's game when there's an ocean swell rolling in from the Atlantic, and I often see up-country fishers emptying their boots after a surprise wave. But trouser waders are the best way to be weather-proof-ish from the waist down. Chesties are OK, but they turn a call of nature into a major performance, especially when it's raining and you have to do a soggy striptease to unsnap the shoulder-straps. A hooded waterproof top's a no-brainer in any conditions – if you don't like the weather, wait twenty minutes, it'll change.

I'm not brand-loyal around clothing, I buy whatever's reduced. I prefer dingy colours – bass don't need racing stripes or logos – and lots of pockets, with at least one that zips closed. (I've seen a good many folk scouring beaches for their car-keys, and I've no wish to join their frantic treasure-hunts.) Spare leads, one to four ounces, live the said jacket pockets. I use bombs if I can, wired leads if I must. In-between patterns like flat sinkers or pyramids strike me as the worst of all worlds: they don't hold in a storm, they don't move in a normal wave, and they're inclined to catch on the sand when there's a decent fish on.

I take two torches, batteries always run out of juice on the darkest nights. Two ciggie lighters and two spools of elastic thread as well, same logic. There's a fleece in each of my packs, wrapped in a plastic bag. I'd rather have one and not need it than start to feel chilly and realise it's by the back door. Hooks aplenty live in my pockets and my surf-fishing bag, which also has a spare spool, a winder of ready-tied leaders, and some twenty-five and forty pound monofilament. A twelve-seater box of assorted lures, a few flies, and some twelve and fifteen test mono form the basis of the little knapsack I take to the rocks or estuaries.

A knife and a sharpening stone are permanent residents in my pockets. In summer I also shove in a wedge, whether I'm planning to use bait or lures – I sometimes see mackerel shoals within casting range. A wad of paper towel never comes amiss: dry fingers are a simple luxury, and clean specs are a health-and-safety issue. (If you can't see where you're going, you wind up on your bottom.)

A few shopping bags are good for collecting your own rubbish, and if you're even remotely public-spirited, other people's shite as well. And on beach-fishing trips I like two types of bait, one fresh and one frozen. Even in a spot where lugworm's a reliable friend, there are days when the bass won't give it a second look, but they'll be all over a razor, a squid, or a sandeel.

A very last thought about tackle and this one should be blindingly obvious, but I run into plenty of fishers who seem to disagree. Look after your gear and keep it decently serviced. I've seen folk whose drags are locked tight with salt and sand, an excellent way to guarantee any decent fish is going to get away. And even if you buy fairly cheap ones like myself, every reel you knacker means fifty-odd quid up the Swanee.

When I finish fishing I loosen the drag right off, and as soon as I'm home the rod and reel have a long shower under the hosepipe followed by a luxury spa treatment using WD-40 and light machine oil. I reckon it's worth paying extra close attention to the roller on the bail-arm, especially if you use braid. A sticky roller quickly develops an evil little groove, and that in turn makes short work of your main-line, leaving it in shreds. Cracked rod-ring liners are another way of cutting the line to pieces.

When I suspect a defective liner I check them all by rubbing them with a cotton bud. And sticking on a new ring's easy enough – well, it's fiddly if you're looking for an elegant two-colour whipping job to match the rest of the set, but I just use any strong nylon thread that comes to hand, followed by a few coats of clear nail varnish. When line becomes tired and tatty I get rid of it in a big hurry. I'm a bit prudent with my money – the polite way of saying I'm as tight as a matador's trousers – but I'm not going to lose a good fish because of worn or banjaxed braid. Every so often I cut off the duffed-up section, usually twenty or thirty yards, then add a bit more thick monofilament backing so the reel's still fairly full.

Hooks need attention as well. With lures and flies everything that's been in the briny goes into an after-use plastic food container. Then it has a thorough rinse at home, a check on the hooks and split-rings, and a generous spritz of WD40 before it goes back into its box for next time. With bait hooks I'm more ruthless. Once they've spent a while in the surf they've earned their keep. I just nip them off and bury them in the compost heap – by the time the grass clippings and vegetable peels are agreeably rotten and mulchy, the steel's rusted away to nothing. Single hooks are dirt cheap, and new ones help me to fish with confidence.

Keeping tackle in good nick costs a few pennies and takes a few minutes, a tiny investment set against the way you'd feel if you hooked a big one and your kit let you down.

• If all the flip-flops that wash up on beaches were put into pairs and recycled, we could eradicate hook-worm in the developing countries.

From a December stir-up and a coloured surf: eleven bass in three hours, the best 5lbs, all on razor. There was ice on the windscreen, but I was too busy to notice my frozen fingers. We're lucky in the far west, the water stays warm year-round – and that's what matters to the fish.

Expensive gear's fine but you don't need it. My rod cost £22 and I love it, it's easy in the hand. The reel seats are a bit cheap-and-nasty, and I usually wind up whipping the reel on with 50lb mono, but the bass don't care. The braid goes for about £20 for 300 metres, and I love it too. The reel (£55) isn't manufactured any more, but I have two spares against the time it wears out. It's big, robust, and hamfisted-plonker-proof; so it'll crank against a hefty pull – pumping's a good way to give slack line and lose fish.

- At the end of an outing I ran into a dog-walker. While we were chatting his dog, a Heinz 57, chewed up my last squid. The fellow apologised profusely and forced the poor mutt to spit out the mangled mouthful. I told him not to worry, I was heading home anyway. Next day a different dog, a fancy wee terrier, scoffed three or four of my squid, and the owner was bit of a plonker about it: 'It's your own fault, that's what dogs do, you should keep your bait in your pocket.' But his karma caught up with his dogma: I saw him in the carpark, trying to clean puke from his passenger seat. Old squid smells bad enough, dog-vomit-squid must really, really pong.

- When the rain starts, some bright spark will tell you it's a passing shower. So what? All showers pass. Noah0's was a passing shower, it just took forty days and forty nights to blow over.

CHAPTER SIX

Rigs for Bass

Taking nothing but his daddy's old bone-grip knife

The angling magazines often run articles on how to build clever rigs – like the clipped-down Pennell-pulley wish-bone rotten-bottom (and yes, I made that one up). The exercise always looks like an A-Level geometry problem and involves enough beads and crimps to create a life-size replica of the crown jewels. And some fishers find the whole thing so complex that they buy ready-assembled rigs. Not for me, I keep it cheap and simple. I'd rather spend my time fishing, not shopping or faffing with bits and pieces.

Lures first. I just put a clip on the end of my braid and Bob's your uncle. I use white braid on my spinning reel, it's almost invisible in the water, so there's no need to tie on a fluorocarbon leader. Less knots, less chance of a knot letting you down – and it's horrible when that happens, you lose a fish and feel like a prat at the same time. A bad hook-hold's bad enough, but a mucked-up Albright can lead to some very expressive terminology as your monster bass swims away with your favourite plug. The only time I use knots at all is when the jelly-fry or the weed-maggots are in. Then I tie a length of fifteen pound mono to the clip, make a bloodknot dropper, and attach a fly two or three feet above the lure. I like the dropper about six inches long, this keeps tangles to a minimum. One key detail: I go for the lightest possible lure-clips. Big beefy ones can interfere with a plug's action.

For fly-fishing, a bit of twelve or fifteen test mono is all it takes, ten feet long in normal weather, down to six when it's hairy. Once in a while I fish two flies, another job for the bloodknot dropper. I see fishers with tapered leaders but I've never bothered. I'm not casting that far and I'm not looking for delicate presentation either, so the mono goes straight to the loop at the end of the fly-line.

In the surf I take some twenty-five pound mono and make a bloodknot with a twelve inch tail and a three foot tail. I like fairly stiff mono – the expensive, limp stuff tends to twist itself in knots in the water. I also like big swivels, not so much for strength, more because they're easy to tie on in the dark. The swivel goes at the top, the weight goes on the shorter tail, the hook or hooks on the longer one. (Looking in the catalogues I think this is a flapper rig, but without all the hardware.) If the tail for the weight's a little on the long side, this makes it easy to change to a bigger or smaller lead as conditions become rougher or calmer; and I shorten the hook length when the sea's wild, to cut down on tangles.

In a total hoolie I switch from twenty-five to forty pound mono, not for strength, but for extra stiffness and less twizzling. When I use razor clam, mussel, mackerel head or side, sandeel, or whole squid, I tie two hooks together, separating them with four to six inches of monofilament. I find this more reliable than a Pennell rig. Otherwise it's one big and brutally sharp hook. I make up a dozen at a time of my probably-flapper rigs and wind them around a spool which lives in my beach bag. So snarled up gear – an eel or just a wild wave – isn't much of a worry. Snip off the old, tie on the new, re-tie the hook and the weight, back in business. And all made that little bit simpler because the swivel isn't some wee gizmo that I can hardly find with cold, numb, spike-scarred fingers.

- I hate wasting bait, and my last cast often carries so much that it looks like a worm flash-mob. But sometimes I take an old packet from the fridge and find nothing but limp corpses. A couple of years back I was making a new vegetable bed, and I took to burying time-expired lugworms and ragworms in the soil. It may be just a coincidence, but my chard plants grew like a rainforest.

Very straightforward stuff, even crude, and if you read the fishing press, that might give you pause. Someone always seems to be chuntering on about how bass are such picky feeders that you need an invisible hook-length of the finest fluorocarbon.

My intuition tells me that's tosh. Bass run from bright lights and thumping bodies, but they have no instinctive fear of translucent string. Even in a calm they aren't put off by a bit of stiff monofilament, and I see flounder-fishers catch bass when their worms are trailing behind things that look like Christmas ornaments designed by colour-blind acid-heads.

Logic tells me it's industrial-strength tosh. After all, a proper bait's a big mouthful with one or two dirty great hooks sticking through it, and that's not exactly subtle. And if you follow the advice of some of the magazine experts (which I don't), your gear arrives in the water after a procedure involving knives, scissors, a baiting needle, and sometimes a bizarre cocktail-making exercise – so not quite the way nature intended. If you're slinging out a crab that's been halved, gutted, de-limbed, and lashed to a ritually mutilated sandeel with a lug or squid garnish, it's very hard to see why you'd use an invisible leader. It would be like nailing a double bacon-cheeseburger to an apple tree to make it look like a naturally-growing treat. Forget fluorocarbon fanciness and finesse, save your pennies. And simple rigs mean your gear's in the water, not laid out on the shore while you rummage for your clips and crimping pliers.

One early spring – when bites are few – I tried a week-long experiment. Two rods in sand-spikes, both baited with lug, both with three ounce bomb weights, both at thirty yards range. One had a running leger with a fluorocarbon hook-length, the other had my normal set-up made from twenty-five pound mono. There was no difference in the number of bites, but the fluorocarbon jobbie had a few more tangles. (The experiment also was a good excuse to fish with my hands in my toasty pockets without feeling like a soft nelly.)

I was fishing in a light surf when I caught a tiny conger, not so much a bootlace, more of a Thai rice noodle. I managed to unhook the horrid little pest without being nipped, but the leader was a proper fankle. I thought about putting on a new rig but I was about to go home, it didn't seem worth it. Instead I nipped off the twisted mono leaving about nine inches of clean stuff. Back on with the hook and some fresh ragworms, and I caught a three-and-half pound bass.

I'd just changed lures, going over to a weightless pinky-brown plastic number, something suggestive of a morbidly obese ragworm. I wanted to make sure it looked OK in the water so I sat on a rock, pulled off half a yard of line, and dropped the softie into the briny. I watched it sink, an appetising go-go-dancer wiggle. Then I put the rod-tip underwater and towed it along. It was engulfed by a three pound bass eighteen inches from the end-ring.

• You can buy lubricant to tighten knots. Or lick the line and save your money.

- If you suffer from wind-knots in your braid – which sound like something caused by too much dietary fibre – try dunking your reel in the water. Line often behaves better when it's damp.

8lb 3oz, whole unwashed squid, November, after a long onshore blow. The friend who took the picture is a proper photographer with proper lenses, and he knows how to make a fish look huge. (My hands really aren't bigger than my head.) The bass took in twelve inches of water. I had to wade out and grab it when it ran aground in a shallower patch.

At the end of a rough spell the water tends to be well coloured, so I like a well-scented bait, usually squid or razor clam. And I almost always use something big and beefy, a high calorie super-sized value-meal.

In a heavy wave the schoolies seem to stay in the deeper water, but the better fish often are very close in. When I'm catching a lot of tiddlers, Plan A is to try a shorter cast. In case you should wonder, Plan B's an even shorter cast.

CHAPTER SEVEN

Adapting to Conditions

You're all just pissing in the wind,
you don't know it but you are.

A lot of fishers go after bass only when conditions look as promising as an investment prospectus crossed with an election manifesto, and I suppose that makes sense. If the surf isn't up to scratch, they chase flatties or light the barbeque and cremate a few burgers. If the wind doesn't look good for fly-casting or lure-fishing for bass they target mullet, wrasse, or cold-boxes full of beer. And some of them use those depressing days on jobs around the house and garden – earning credit with their families so they'll have no problem bunking off when the weather turns. Subject to current regulations I go bass fishing at any time of year, in good conditions or bad. Stuff the DIY, stuff the weeds, I need my regular outings. In early summer I have the odd bash at gilthead bream or seatrout, and in winter I fluke a few codling, but these are by-catch. I always fish in a way that gives me a good shot at a bass, and if something else should happen to oblige, that's just a bonus – as long as it isn't a weever or a conger. In the far west we have a few bass around all year long. February to April can be hard, and it's no time to be keeping fish when they're spawning, but it's not a lost cause. In late winter traditional lure fishing falls off like a tight-rope walker with vertigo, but it isn't a complete bust. A sandeel shad in the surf-table can do the trick even in March. And bait-fishing never really lets up. It slows down in the chilly months – when I wear enough fleeces to look like a Michelin man with a puncture – but it keeps ticking over.

Two good things about bass fishing year-round. One, unlike the cod brigade I don't head out in winter with a load that would produce a hernia in a keep-fit camel – tripods, shelters, heaters, and what-have-you. And two, I've learned how to give myself a decent chance of catching bass in all sorts of weathers and sea-states. So let's look at how you can approach your fishing whatever the conditions, starting with the sublime and working down to the gor-blimey.

But first a word about tides. Some folk see the tide table as a fishing agony-aunt's self-help manual for life, the answer to all embarrassing bass-related problems: use a good moisturiser, drink more water, and only hit this mark over slack high. I don't worry that much about the state of the tide. Bass feed anyway, they just move around as the level rises and falls.

Knowing your areas means knowing where to fish at high or low, on the make or on the drop. The size of the tide makes more difference than the state of the tide – small neaps generally give slow fishing, and that's character-building at best. But in or out, ebbing or flowing, you can find feeding bass anyway. For example a nearby beach has a reputation for going well only on the second half of the drop. It's a very gently sloping strand, and here's what I've noticed: fishers cast to the third wave, then the tide ebbs away. After fifteen minutes and a lugworm-tainted sandwich, they have bites. Why?

Because the bass on this mark generally feed in about eighteen inches of water, so the time spent scoffing that bait-smeared snack is the time it takes for the surf to become shallower. On a making tide a cast that was too long to begin with is a no-hoper, however much insanitary food they nibble, as two feet of depth turns into three. I fish the beach at all states of the tide. On the ebb I start with a thirty yard lob, on the flow about twenty yards. Rising or falling, my catches are the same.

Another beach is known to be a high water spot. I've made good catches over the top, right in front of the carpark. But I've done even better when the water's out, the difference being that the feeding bass tend to be in the gullies at the other end, away to the east; and a lot of fishers are too heavy-laden – or maybe too bone lazy – to fancy a mile-long plodge along the sand, so they stay close to their cars and blank. A third beach is popular around low water when there's a set of breakers as good-looking as a Hollywood superstar in soft focus. At high tide there's just a plug ugly dump. But the fishing's almost as good as long as the fisher casts really short, right to the back of the one and only wave.

One of my lure and fly spots can be crowded when the tide's coming up from low. There's a swipe of current which swirls small fish, crabs, and prawns from the weed, the predator version of a motorway food court where they offer every fattening food you can imagine, pizza to burgers to fried chicken. At high water I have the place to myself, just me and the bass which cruise the shore like over-eager traffic wardens, sucking down weed maggots and finger mullet.

In truth nearly all my spots deliver at any stage of the tide – as long as you move around and adjust to the conditions. The pull of the moon may bring out skinny-dippers and drunken surfers, but the bass keep biting anyway. And now on to dealing with the vagaries of wave and weather.

- Do you ever wonder who eats supermarket mackerel?

Ideal lure-fishing

I love a moderate onshore breeze, just enough to make the water bubbly, a baitfish jacuzzi. If the sea's warm enough for sandeels or little mackerel I often start out with shallow-divers or top-water lures. They don't snag up too much, and in the half-light it's great fun to see fish hit on or near the surface – even a modest bass can make a swirling splash like an uncoordinated springboard diver with a skinful of beer. A lot of lure-maniacs reckon you need your surface plug to be walking the dog, lots of to-ing and fro-ing. With a decent chop I seem to have just as many takes with an irregular but almost constant retrieve. I let the wave add the herky-jerky bits and leave the dog-walking to the Kennel Club.

Another thing I see a good deal is an obsession with distance. Athletic-looking types will clamber out to the very tip of a promontory or wade as far as they dare, then sling their lure miles out into the blue yonder. I'm sure it feels satisfying to stand on a precarious rock and watch a plug hurtling towards the Americas, and tackle advertisements tend to show photos of fishers doing exactly that. But the feeding fish generally are really close to shore. Bass come around rocks because that's where the food's concentrated and easy to grab, so a monster cast can be a cast too far.

When I chat with practitioners of the almighty fling they tell me most of their hits come at the end of the retrieve. They believe bass follow the lure all the way in, then attack only when it seems to be escaping into the shallows. And maybe they're right, but I can't see why a bass is going to waste precious energy chasing its prey from pillar to post. Why not just munch it right away, then find another snack as quickly and easily as possible? I reckon long-range lures swim unnoticed and unmolested until they arrive in the feeding zone, and that's when they're attacked. The deeper, stiller water beyond the waves is like the fishy high-street, I'd say, good for travel. The churned up stuff right around the snags is like the corner kebab shop, great for tucking into a fattening bellyful of grub; and that's where hungry predators are going to lurk. So when I feel like trying to send my lure into orbit I aim it at thirty or forty-five degrees to the water's edge. And I always fish it right back to the rod-tip.

People also bang on about animating a lure, moving it as soon as it hits the briny, but I sometimes have a hit on a fly or a plug before it's in motion. I think bass are attracted by the entry splash, then persuaded to have a go by the way it wobbles, like a bashed-up tiddler on its last legs – and a dying fry or sandeel is the last word in easy eating, irresistible. When I start retrieving, my first approach is a slow, slightly stop-start affair, one turn of the reel or eighteen inches of fly-line per second. If that's no good I'll go slower; and faster, speeding up until the lure almost jumps out of the water. If there's still nothing doing I'll try a different fly, plug, spoon, or shad, or a move along the shore.

Colder water calls for low-and-slow, a lure near the bottom moving like a terminally tired tortoise on tranquilisers. In my spots this usually means a weedless soft plastic or a grub-shaped fly, fished almost as if it were a free-lined bait. It's easy to think that an artificial needs a bit of movement, but the sin of sloth can be deadly for the bass, so I just let my flies and softies sink with the odd tweak, or fish them in glacially slowly. Sometimes in cool conditions I use a flying condom or a jointed diving plug, black and silvery white to suggest a little mullet, with a pedestrian retrieve. Cheap lures are a good idea for this style of fishing unless you want to leave all your pocket money hung up on the reefs.

Early April, but it felt like January in Siberia, my ears were stinging by the time I arrived in my little cove. The tide was high, two feet of water over the biggest of the rocks and weed patches. I knew my hands would be like frozen fish-fingers, so I already had my lure clipped on, a soft plastic stick-bait in Ayu, a gungy lugworm colour. Not much wave, so I made my first cast ten feet back from the edge, then I stuffed my left hand in my pocket to warm it up a bit. Bang, a fish on, about two pounds. Back it went, I checked the lure, and out with another cast. Hand restored to the pocket as the softie sank through the water, then a twitch and half a pace backwards, the Motown back-up singer shuffle – without the hand-claps. Another twitch, another step. Then a second take, a three pounder, ideal for lunch. After my third fish I faced the truth: my feet were numb, my eyes were streaming, and my right hand was aching with cold. Enough fun for one day, I could hear the siren song of the car-heater.

Rough as rats lure-fishing

I notice folk out on rock marks in hideous hooters, waves like super-tankers crashing in. Not for me. I've seen too many people get in trouble, and I'm older, wiser, and less nimble than I used to be. I take no chances. I'm sometimes told, 'If anything happens, I can call for help on my mobile.' I don't think so. When a hundred tons of water batter you against the shore, you're not going to be calling anyone but Saint Peter. Besides, what gives a pleasure-fisher the right to ask RNLI and helicopter crews to head out in life-threatening conditions? They'd do it, for sure, but they shouldn't have to, not just because some nitwit has stuff-all common-sense and even less consideration for others.

Anyway lure-fishing doesn't have to be from rocks. In the old days – when we still called it spinning, before the red rods and pricey plugs came along – we'd stand on beaches and chuck Toby or Koster spoons into the surf. Mostly it was a way of amusing ourselves while we waited for bites on our beach-rods, but those spoons caught a few good bass. Nowadays I'll sling out a wedge and fish it in with a pumping action, planing up and fluttering down. If the beach is really flat I go with a sandeel shad bumped slowly along the bottom. Whether it's a wedge or a shad I often have a take when the lure's almost at my feet. I had a six pound bass on a shad from less than a foot of water. It grabbed the lure, took off about ten yards of line, then ran aground on a slightly raised lump of sand.

- Bass scales make a decent free slow-release fertiliser, and they help break up heavy soil.

- When I tell people I'm using squid baits, their noses wrinkle. Call it calamari and they smack their lips. Apparently the Italian for ragworm is *verme marino predatore*, but that doesn't seem to have the same appetising effect.

Rougher than wire-haired giant cane-rats lure-fishing

If it's too wild to chuck a lure from the safety of a beach, I'm heading for an estuary or a sea-pool. Streams that hardly even show up on the Ordnance Survey map often are bass magnets. They're full of baby fish, crabs, and prawns being swept around in the current, predator pig-out heaven. These spots are shallow, just a foot or so of water, so sometimes I use a small top-water plug. Generally I go with the fly-rod, a floating line, and a fry-type fly or a palmer-dressed shrimpy effort, size 2 down to size 8. Casting's hairy in wild weather, but there's no call for distance in a sea-pool. And I never fish without my specs and my woolly hat (Cornish health-and-safety kit), so out-of-control back-casts aren't going to wind up in my eyes or ears.

The wind was out of the west, gusting to force seven, and there was wrack on all my beaches. So I tried the mouth of an apparently nameless brook, starting about an hour before low water and first light. I put on a size 6 teal-blue-and-silver and

*made a couple of short casts – none of that double-haul stuff,
it was hard enough just to stand up in the gale. On the second
chuck as the line swung around in the current it stopped and I
heard a splash. A seatrout of about two pounds, so back it went.
(I have a licence for migratory fish, but I can't bring myself to
kill them.) After the seatrout's leaping I rested the pool for a few
minutes. Then a few more flicks and I was into a small bass.
Returned again, and another break.*

*By now it was getting light and I was hoping for a second
bass. I love it when you see the fish turn and chase the fly,
it's heart-stopping. Anyway the tide had slackened, so I was
whipping the fly along the surface when from the corner of my
eye I saw something land on top of it, a big splash. 'Oh spit,'
I thought, 'must be a seagull.' But no, it was a flounder, the
hook nicked into its underside. I've had a few more flatties on
flies and on top-water jobs, and almost all of them have belly-
flopped onto the lure. Athletic little chaps, especially for fish
shaped like pudgy tea-plates.*

- I was walking on a pier in the summer when a toddler dropped
a hot-dog. His dad promised the nipper a replacement, then
chucked the grubby snack into the water. Immediately a bass of
four or five pounds swam up and grabbed it. I feel I should learn
something from this, but I'm not sure the fishing world is ready
for a pork-sausage lure. Maybe it's just the word 'sausage' that
strikes a wrong note. How about a Labrax Cumberland Bass-
Banger, twenty pounds for a packet of six?

Flat-as-a-dab lure-fishing

Generally this is a summertime challenge and it can be a real
blighter. In a calm I'll often see decent bass cruising close to the
shore, and they'll follow a lure, just to get my hopes up. But they'll
turn away at the last minute like wine snobs sniffing snootily at a
glass of cheap plonk.

101

Two things sometimes work the oracle. One's to try by night with a swimming plug, a flying condom, a little grub-shaped fly, or a weightless soft plastic, and to fish very slowly indeed. With a plug or a flying condom I crank only fast enough to feel a slight vibration from the lure, and with a fly or a softie it's just the odd twitch now and again.

The other approach, if the light's up, is to use small lures and crank like a demented pastry chef on a meringue-whisking binge. A twenty gramme Toby retrieved so fast it's almost flying out of the water has saved me a lot of blanks. To go even smaller I tie a bloodknot into a length of mono, put a fry-like fly or a muddler on the dropper, just about anything on the point, and again crank the reel at warp speed.

My theory's that a bass, even if it's not feeding, has an involuntary reflex to snap at any morsel flying past its nose – the same way children can't drive past a fast-food outlet without a rest-stop. And if the lures still don't do any good I'll scour the pools for shrimp or a goby, then free-line it or pop it under a float. The fundamentalist lure-purists may disapprove, but a flapping live-bait works on bass the way a bacon roll works on me – they'll scoff it even if they're completely full.

Late May, breezes from the north-east. According to the old rhyme this is a combination of when the canny angler goes not forth (north) and when the fish bite least (east). But I'd heard reports of seatrout jumping in Mount's Bay, so I took my lure-fishing gear to a shingle beach an hour before the dawn. The tide was slack high and the water was glassy.

I started off with a black flying condom, a lure I like for prospecting, when I don't know what sort of baitfish are around. As the light came up I managed a mullet, and I lost a seatrout when it jumped and shed the hook. (I always return seatrout, but this wasn't a long-distance release – it came off after its first run.) So I walked along the shingle, scanning the water. Then I heard a swirl, a heavyweight boxer doing an underwater uppercut in a bathtub. I squatted to stop myself being outlined against the sky and watched the margin.

After a while I noticed some little disturbances, finger mullet, then another great sucking splash. I wiped my specs, and there was a bass, almost motionless a yard out from the water's edge. My fingers were shaking like frankfurters in an earthquake, but I managed to unclip the flying condom and put on a big soft plastic job with a black back and a silvery-white belly.

Still squatting, I lobbed it along the beach six feet up-current of the bass. There was a swirl as the bass flicked its tail, and my first thought was that I'd cast too close and scared her off. But no, a tweak, another swirl, and my rod came alive. Seven-and-a-quarter pounds. She made me feel a lot better about the seatrout.

- It was the height of the tourist season, and I was casting lures at first light. I paused to answer a call of nature, lowered my waders, unzipped, and set about my business. Then I saw 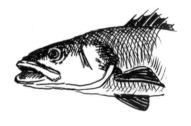 a big old boil in the water, three or four sandeels skittering. I grabbed my rod, dropped a plug right in the middle of the eddy, and immediately I was into a fair bass. By the time it was ready to be beached I thought I could hear voices behind me. A quick glance over my shoulder confirmed it: three hikers on the cliff path, binoculars aimed in my direction. At this point I realised that my waders were still down, my fly was open, and my trouser-tackle was out in the fresh air. I landed, unhooked, and returned that bass without ever turning around; and I'm sure some holiday folk are still confused as to why Cornish fishers buy waist-waders and wear them round their knees. But at least they don't think we're flashers.

- I remember an old Scotsman who worked on a salmon river. On dry, warm, sunny, fishless days he'd look at the sky and say, 'Terrible weather for folk.' A three beat pause. 'Good for the tourists though.'

Bass can be thin on the ground in the spring, but I fancied some fillets fried in crumbs, so I bounced a sandeel shad in the surf-table and caught one about 55cm, perfect eating size and fat as butter. It grabbed the lure, ran a little way, then became stranded, beached on a ridge in the sand.

Lure-fishers often look for steep drop-offs, but I find bass feed better in the shallows. As long as their backs are covered they seem to do very well for themselves. Thinner water means less room for the prey to get away or hide, so easier hunting for predators.

Late December, the wind was howling and there was weed on nearly all my regular spots. I fished a shallow sea-pool, 9-18 inches deep, with my old trout rod and a floating seven-weight line. A 4lb bass took a home-tied fly on a size 2 hook, something to suggest a whitebait or a small sandeel, stripped fast through the surface. Tying flies saves me a fair few quid, and it's a good way to keep thinking about bass when the weather's too filthy to chase them. You can spend an arm and a leg on fly gear but you really don't need to.

The fly can be a good way to deal with water too shallow for anything else – and even a half-way decent bass is great fun on light gear, especially when you see the bow-wave coming at the fly.

- If all the money we fritter away on tackle and bait were turned into fish at fishmongers' prices, we'd be eating seafood three or four times a day. Imagine what that would do to marine stocks. So whenever you have a lousy outing you should congratulate yourself on a good conservation effort. Don't think of it as blanking, it's sustainable fishing.

Winter lure-fishing

Once in a while the weather's fit for plugging from the rocks in winter, but lures near the surface don't do the business for me. I prefer to go much deeper and slower than that. A jointed plug's one option, wandering along near the bottom – a cheap one, so it's OK if it snags. A weedless soft plastic's another, twitched ever so slightly. But generally my winter lure-fishing's from beaches where I bounce a shad across the sand in the surf-table. When it's chilly this lets me keep one hand in my pocket, just shuffle backwards up the strand like a slow-motion Michael Jackson, one glove out in the weather, tweaking the rod as I go. And it fetches me a few bass – along with all sorts of by-catch, from codling to flounders. There's almost nothing that won't have a go at a sandeel shad. I've had rays and dogfish as well, all from less than three feet of water.

Ideal bait-fishing

On the flattish beaches I prefer I look for a set of 2-6 waves, a height of 2-6 feet. Surfers like a clean wave, but I go for what they call messy surf, no elegant curl, lots of foamy breakers – no directionally challenged youngsters in wetsuits, lots of sloppy push-and-pull.

This calls for my bog-standard set-up, a three or four ounce bomb weight, a hook-length of three feet, and a cast that puts my bait into the frothiest area of the surf. I've read that bass lurk in bubbly water because it contains extra oxygen. Maybe so, but I reckon it's all about easy eating. White horses aerate the whole ocean, but when it's fizzy in the shallows that means swirls on the sea floor. And a stir-up provides a calorie-laden bass bonanza as worms and razor clams wash from the sand, crabs and sandeels are bashed around in the tow, and dead fish and squid are pushed onshore.

That's why short casts are effective. How short? Sometimes I'll try a long heave then fish my gear back to the sand a few yards at a time; and generally I find my fish not far from my boots.

Late July, a few days of south-west winds and heavy showers. (As we tell the summer visitors every year, this is very unusual.) Anyway the upshot was a lovely surf, fizzy and busy. I was on the beach before dawn tossing lugworms into the froth. I rarely catch big bass in July, but I had five in an hour, the best about three pounds. I kept that one and sat on my backpack stool for a smoke.

Then I saw a small figure approaching. No tripod, no headlamp, perhaps a fellow-member of demented bass fishers anonymous. It was a youngster from Holland, Jan, and he'd fished all night for one flounder. He was using lug, no problem there, and a sensible weight, three or four ounces. 'How far out are you fishing?' 'As far as I can,' he told me, 'but I'm not so much good at casting.' I suggested a fresh bait and a twenty-five metre lob.

Before I'd even lit my dart the lad was shouting, 'Fish, I'm in the fish.' It was a fat beauty, almost four pounds. Jan tied it to his tackle-bag and told me he was going up to his parents' caravan. He'd wake them up with a bass breakfast. So help me, I tried to persuade him that most non-fishers are somewhat sane, they enjoy their sleep, they prefer breakfast a bit later than four-thirty. If he took heed, I'm glad. And if he didn't, this is a belated apology to Jan's Mum and Dad.

It was a perfect morning, August, an onshore breeze, three or four sets of breakers, a left-over from the previous week's storms. I was on a beach that – until the winter gales of 2013 – fished especially well over low water. The sand developed a pool at half tide and as the ebb moved out it emptied the pool through a shallow channel. As the run-off drained, it carried worms and crabs out into the surf, a Michelin-starred swim-through bass belly-buster. Arriving on the strand I met a couple of chaps who were leaving. But for the weight of their waders they'd have been walking on air: half a dozen bass between them.

So I was confident as I lobbed a lugworm bait thirty yards into the foam, and sure enough I was almost straight into a fish. About fifteen inches, a legal keeper at the time, but not big enough to be any use.

Second cast, same story, a twin. Then a triplet, then a quadruplet. 'Blimey,' I thought, 'I'm going to run through all my bait without a proper eater.' So a shorter cast, fifteen yards, dropping the lead into a foot or so of water. Five minutes later I had a three pounder at my feet. Then another. With my last bait I flicked my gear out about five yards, just inside the first breaking wave, and a five pound bass snaffled it.

It was May and I was on a north-facing beach that's often covered with razor clam shells. The surf was bubbling, and I thought I had a chance of some bass and maybe a gilthead. I tied on a fat razor and lobbed it out. Not a sausage. Try a few lugworms. Not a chipolata, not a cocktail sausage. Then I noticed a squelching sound as I walked. I turned on my torch and saw the shore was carpeted with one inch jelly fry. I searched my bag and pockets for a small hook, but the best I managed was a short-shank 3/0. It took about twenty of the tiny fry, speared through their heads, to make a decent mouthful, and I reckoned a firm cast would send the little so-and-sos flying from the hook.

So a ten yard lob and I waited. In two or three minutes I was into a bass. I spent most of the dawn hours on my knees, collecting fry and impaling them. And when I was walking to the car I ran into a woman with a spaniel. She looked at my fish bag. 'So it worked,' she said. 'I was watching you kneeling on the sand. All that time you spent praying for a fish, your prayers were answered.'

Of course Murphy's Law reigns supreme, so there's a common snag with a good wave. Especially after a calm spell it can drag in a load of weed. Some fishers react with a blast of choice expletives and a swift return to the carpark. Not so fast, I say, teach me a few new words if you must, but don't give up right away. If the weed's floating around, try moving. Weed tends to travel in belts or clumps, so a fifty-yard hike can take you from a morass of the wretched stuff to clearer water.

Another thing that sometimes works is to fish a really flat beach where the breeze is blowing directly into your face. A stiff onshore wind can push all the flotsam into the shallows or onto the sand, so you may be standing on mats of junk but finding a wave that's quite fishable. If the weed's on the bottom – frondy, thick-stalked kelp often seems to sink and stay put – then I use a weight that grips the sand rather than rolling around gathering snags. It's not as good as a moving sinker for finding bass but at least it keeps the bait in the water.

A lot of folk love a good surf at the end of an onshore hoolie. Me too – I also, to show respect to my old English teacher – but the fishing can be even livelier at the very beginning of the blow, just as the wave's starting to build and before the water colours properly. I reckon bass have an instinct that tells them when the weather's on the turn. Maybe they sense barometric pressure, maybe they're cannier than the boffins at the Met Office. Either way they often seem to move onto the beach in good time for the feeding bonanza, like shopaholics camping out on the pavement ahead of the Harrods sale. And the front end of a storm sometimes lets you fish before the worst of the weed shows up.

- Whenever I hear a politician spouting numbers I think of the words of Andrew Lang: this is someone 'who uses statistics as a drunken man uses a lamp-post – for support rather than illumination.'

Rough as rats bait-fishing, and even rougher

In a genuinely heavy sea there's no option but to use a wired lead. When the surf's like an industrial dish-washer with a bad attitude, a bomb weight doesn't wander, it flies up the beach as fast as a surfer with a wetsuit full of stinging jellyfish. I also use a shorter hook-length – down from three feet to eighteen or even twelve inches – and sometimes a heavier monofilament rig to cut down on tangles. And a really large bait. Even in a moderate sea I go for a proper portion of nourishing treats, something at least as big as a couple of fat fingers.

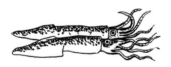 *Mid-October, an onshore gale. I arrived on the beach at the same time as another fellow. He tried one cast, then told me he was moving to a more sheltered spot where he'd be able to get his gear out further. I fished a big whole squid – a ten incher – at fifteen or twenty yards range. There were six or seven sets of breakers, and my bait was just outside the nearest one. In about an hour I had a seven or eight pounder (released) and one of 11lbs 2oz. Especially in rough conditions a lot of fishers think their bait needs to be beyond the white water. I fare best when I fish the really shallow, really wild surf-table.*

Generally I use bomb weights, but a hooting storm and a crashing surf call for a switch to a wired sinker. Also a shorter hook-length, to avoid too many tangles.

In a stir-up I can't see how a bass is going to find anything that small, so I like a half mackerel, a large squid, a mess of razor clam – a proper eye-full with a good strong scent. When it's really rough I see fishers making long casts, trying to put their baits beyond the wild water. 'Nothing could swim in that, never mind feed,' they'll say. And I reckon that's half right. Schoolies seem to steer clear of a vicious wave, but for bigger bass, no problem. Even when the undertow pulls like a randy rock-star, you'll still be in with a chance of a chunky fish.

- Whopper, whopping, the verb must be 'to whop'. As in, 'I whopped a big bacon sandwich' (transitive), or, 'That squid really whops' (intransitive).

My only computer bookmarks are for weather and surf sites. Before I head out I check three or four, but even when they all agree they're wrong half the time. This was how it worked out one December. The breeze was to be cross-shore, moderate, the surf up to five feet. That was the cyber-story. Then the real thing, a stiff onshore breeze, the biggest breakers about nine feet. I was on a flat beach, so to be safe I had to set up twenty yards back and my gear was going twenty yards beyond the water's edge, right into the middle of the dump. Even with braid the wave-drag was as strong a steroid-enhanced weightlifter and I was jogging up and down the beach to keep the line tight, aerobics in trouser-waders.

What's more the only bait I'd brought – thanks to the forecasters, whose technology seems to be a million pound pine-cone – was ragworm and sandeel. So I was cramming as many worms as I could fit onto a 4/0 hook and hoping for the best. At first light a dog-walker beetled up. 'There won't be any bass in that lot,' he said with that snide, know-it-all tone of a bank-manager turning down a business plan.

As he spoke I felt a pull, then slack line, and I tightened into what felt like a good fish. The water was so roiled that the bass was swimming at random. One minute it was running and stripping line, the next it was flying towards me and I was cranking and trotting backwards at the same time. It weighed in at seven-and-three-quarter pounds. I had two more from the same distance before my worm ran out.

Late summer, we were in the middle of a series of southerly gales, and Mount's Bay looked like a mad scientist's water feature with a V-8 engine. I drove from beach to beach, hoping to find a place where I might be able to put a bait into the briny at least; but one was too rough for safety, the next was knee-deep in weed. Finally I thought of a spot that's sheltered by a couple of reefs half a mile offshore. It's a bit of a hike, but I plodged along the sand in the wind and the rain and I thought the sea was moderating as I went. Not a lot, but an eight foot wave is a sight friendlier than a twelve-footer. The water was so churned up that a big smelly bait was the only way to go, so on with two unwashed squid and a wired lead. Casting as hard and as low as I could into the howling wind I thought my gear was winding up in the crunch of the second breaker, and that was the second of eight or nine.

Now the one good thing about wind is that it lets you turn your back, put up your hood, and stay at least a little bit dry. So I stood there in the gale listening to the raindrops hammering against my once-allegedly-waterproofs, feeling my braid bouncing in the weather. A very slight pluck, like a small piece of weed, another one, and then my gear headed off towards the Scillies.

Generally I find bass don't pull much in a really churned-up sea, but this one broke the pattern. She took fifteen minutes to land and she went seven-and-a-half pounds. Back at the car I ran into another fisher. 'Wasting your time in this weather,' he told me helpfully, 'You should try for a mullet inside the harbour.'

It was mid-December and we'd had a few days of wild weather. I was on an exposed beach, the waves were between six and eight feet, sixty-odd yards of white water. The wind had moderated but it was still gusting to thirty knots. When I arrived I saw that the western end of the beach was carpeted with fronds of kelp, so I hoofed it for half a mile and

111

found some clear water. Clear of weed and just about clear of fish: two hours for a tiny schoolie and a microscopic flounder. Then at first light I saw a gigantic island made of wrack. It was the size of a rugby pitch and it was surrounded by duck-diving cormorants, a sure sign of a bass mega-larder. I tried to drop my crab bait ten feet down-tide of the weed, but if you've ever seen one of those accurate casting demonstrations, I was not the bod-with-a-rod. Two weights lost to the wrack in very short order, but the better casts led to bites almost as my gear hit the water. I wound up with six bass, the best four-and-a-bit pounds.

- My grandfather was a parish priest and I grew up well steeped in the King James Bible. As a result I have odd bits of scripture to suit a lot of fishing situations. Wake up to a hoolie: 'A sound from heaven as of a mighty rushing wind.' (Acts 2:2) Toss a few dead ragworms into the wave: 'Cast thy bread upon the waters.' (Ecclesiastes 11:1) Watch the surf die away: 'He maketh the storm a calm.' (Psalms 107:29) Feel a bite: 'Now the Lord had prepared a great fish.' (Jonah 1:17) And best of all, land a whopper: 'Canst thou draw out leviathan with an hook?' (Job 41:1)

Flat-as-a-dab bait-fishing

With a calm forecast I used to leave my beach gear at home and fish fly, lures, or a prawn or blenny if I could catch one. Then there was a spell when my lure-fishing spots were banjaxed by weed or mud – but the beaches were clear. People tell me I'm wasting my time – pissing in the wind-less-ness – when I cast my bait into a tiny ripple, but I've had some fair catches. And here's what makes the difference.

First, I use small weights. My beach rod's rated for two to four ounces, but I go as low as one ounce to encourage my bait to move about a bit. No problem, because the second tactic's to fish really close in, as short as two or three yards from the water's edge. Third, I find my fish not on shallow sand but on steeply shelving beaches with cross-flows, so the current pushes food along and builds it up against the ledges and drop-offs. Fourth, I use clear water sight-baits, usually energetic ragworms or a monster sandeel. A free-lined live-bait's another option.

I hook the fish a little aft of amidships and lob it in. Then I keep tightening the line, which turns the bait so it's heading out to sea and makes it swim away. If I can't catch a live-bait, I sometimes try half a mackerel or a squid, also with no weight. It may not cast that well but no worry, the fish feed within feet of the water's edge. And finally, stay away from the margin – at least ten yards back – and avoid bouncing around like Tigger at a heavy-metal gig. In a glassy calm bass can be very leery.

- I took some friends to visit a garden by an estuary. I went for a wander by the water, and in the shallows I spotted three cruising bass. The smallest must have been six pounds. And my gear was at home. That was a long morning.

A mid-summer morning in a heatwave, I planned on fishing from about three o'clock until first light. There was barely a ripple on the water, and the air was muggy after a heavy thundershower. I walked along the beach thirty feet back from the waterline, tossing a bunch of frisky ragworms and a one ounce sinker into about two feet of glassy calm. But it was slow going: one schoolie and one small flounder – or maybe a plaice.

Then the light came up and I could see the problem. The water was soupy from the rainstorm – cream soup, not consommé. Winter rainwater run-off can really stuff up the fishing, it lowers the sea temperature in the shallows and the bass move off. In warm weather not such a problem, but cloudy water makes a sight bait like ragworm hard to find. So off with the weight, on with a pair of 6/0 hooks and a ten inch squid, and a gentle lob.

First cast, as the bait hit the water I saw a swirl like a breast-stroking sumo wrestler doing a racing turn. A few seconds later I felt a thump, then the line started to peel off the reel. I closed the bail-arm and seven bells broke loose. By the time the fish came to hand I had a gallery of three dog-walkers and seven assorted mutts. The bass went eight-and-a-half pounds.

- When I was a nipper I missed out on a lot of fishing because I found bait-digging so exciting that I just couldn't stop.

- People tell me I should take a flask of coffee and some sandwiches on my fishing trips. A rotten idea, if I had a full tummy and a hot drink I'd forget to come home.

I caught a decent eater, about three pounds, from a flat calm morning in December. The water was close to 12 degrees, the air was well below zero. I don't enjoy lures or the fly when it's really cold: you have to keep both hands out in the weather. Bait-fishing lets you shove one into a pocket. I used 20-odd head-hooked ragworms – as many as would fit onto a 4/0 – fished with no weight at all in about nine inches of water. I'd guess my bait was only 20 feet out.

I reckon it's always good to be reasonably stealthy on the shore – no light on the wave, no dancing hippopotamus impressions. In flat conditions it's vital to keep still and away from the water's edge.

And it's never completely hopeless if you're prepared to try something different.

Warm and windless weather in July, the wave was less than a foot – more a ripple than a wave. Other people often tell me I'm wasting my time in these conditions, and a calm sea certainly can make for tough fishing. But that doesn't mean you're bound for a boring blank – as long as you adapt.

I used a one-and-a-half ounce bomb with a big tangle of lashing ragworms, fished at about ten yards range on a shelving beach. Five decent bass, the best, somewhere around eight pounds. I didn't weigh it, I just used the length converter.

In a small surf – or no surf at all – I like a sight bait, a short cast, a light weight, and to stand very well back from the water, ten yards or so. A flattish sea is the one thing that'll send me in search of a steep shore-line.

Late July, flat calm with a steady drizzle, typical UK summer weather. I was fishing a shelving beach with a decent swipe of tide, hoping the current might make up for the lack of a wave. It didn't, two hours for one small flounder. Then at dawn I saw patches of dimpled water. Probably mackerel, so I took off the bait tackle and tied on a forty gramme wedge. (A wedge lives in my pocket in the summer, just in case.) My beach-rod's light enough to chuck forty grammes a respectable distance, and it didn't take long to deliver a couple of fat mackerel. 'Hold the bacon roll, here's breakfast,' I thought, now what about a live-bait? Another few slings with the wedge, another one pound-ish mackerel. OK, it seemed the whole shoal was about the same size, way too big to cast even with a gentle lob.

I put on a 6/0 hook, nipped it through the mackerel's back just behind the dorsal fin, and opened the bail-arm. I held the rod in my left hand and made a right-handed toss with the mackerel. I was never any good at cricket, it flew about ten feet and touched down with a splosh like a clumsy water-skier's face-plant. But by holding the rod high and twitching the line I managed to persuade my live-bait to keep swimming out to sea.

It was about twenty yards out when I felt a thump – a hoodlum bass mugging its victim. Line ran from the spool, then stopped, then off again faster. I closed the bail-arm and my rod assumed the position, bent over in a hoop. Bass often seem to fight harder in really flat water, this one was a case in point: fifteen minutes to land, three-and-a-half pounds.

- Waders only spring leaks on cold, wet days. A double dose of Murphy's Law.

*High summer, sunny days and windless nights, so I thought
I'd try lure-fishing from an exposed north coast beach.
It's a board-riders' mecca, it always holds onto some wave.
But not today, a nine inch ripple, no use to any surfer bigger
than a malnourished squirrel. What's more as I drove north my
shoulder locked up – I think it's bursitis, not very painful, but
it makes repeated casting pretty uncomfortable. So onto Plan
B, the spinning rod with a one ounce weight and a bunch of
ragworms. Even with such a small sinker the surf wasn't moving
my gear, so I was twitching it along, almost like floundering with
a baited spoon. And it worked: three bass, small, but fun on the
light gear.*

*As I wandered along I ran into a pair of chaps from South
Africa. They'd popped into a local tackle-shop and been kitted
up with beach-casting outfits, they were chucking big grip-
weights and peeler crabs fifty yards into the millpond. And their
faces had that glazed look: in cricket fans it says rain-stopped-
play, in fishers it says long-term-blanking. Luckily my jacket
doubles as a sporting goods store, so I offered them a couple of
small weights and a few ragworms. 'But how would I cast it out,
man?' asked one, 'This rod's specified for four to eight ounces.'
'If it'll go twenty yards, you'll be fine.' When they'd had three or
four schoolies one of them toddled off to their camper-van.*

*Fifteen minutes later he was back, accompanied by a
wonderful smell. 'I'm not going to insult you by offering to pay
for the weights and worms,' he said, 'but a bacon sandwich
might be in order.'*

- Up close a ragworm's a scary creature, like something from a
low budget science-fiction film. When the fishing's slow you can
learn some weird stuff.

- Why a few good outings don't mean you've cracked it –
statistical wisdom from one of my daughter's professors: 'The
plural of anecdote is not data.'

11lbs 5oz, December, in an onshore gale, along with two six-pounders. Bait was two fat razor clams, a good choice in very coloured water. I was casting about 15 yards into eighteen inches of foam. Another chap (somehow) was casting 80-odd yards. He had lots of fish, but all schoolies.

Big bass are often a good deal closer in than fishers believe possible.

Winter bait-fishing

The only differences I find when I fish bait in the cold months are that the bass seem to be later to come on the feed, and that scent baits often fare better than sight baits.

In warm conditions I like to be on the shore a couple of hours before the first hint of dawn, but winter bass go better from just a wee bit before sunrise until it's as light as it's going to be. I'm not sure why. Maybe the angle of the sun means winter rays don't penetrate the water much, maybe it's because the nights are so long and the days so short, or maybe bass – like fishers – appreciate what little heat comes with the morning light. No complaints anyway, chilly weather's good for an extra hour of duvet-diving.

I find also that winter's the time for baits that put some juice into the water even if it's gin-clear: lugworm, razor, squid, mussel, mackerel head. I suspect big bass move less briskly when it's cold, like most of us creaky-jointed codgers. They seem to stay tighter to the bottom as well, and this makes it easier for them to find food with a scent trail.

A week before Easter, the water was eleven or twelve degrees. I was on the beach before five but it was as slow as an arthritic tree sloth so I took a wander. In the middle of the sand I saw a new scour, maybe eighteen inches deep and as big as an Olympic swimming pool. It was jammed with weed, crabs, and shells. This was a hungry scavenger's paradise, a detox fat farm in reverse, an open invitation to an all-you-can-eat scoff-athon. When the tide came up a bit, I reckoned the bass would be flooding in for a graze. About six o'clock I could see the biggest waves were washing in, so I lobbed my mussels ten yards into the channel that was filling the scour. Between six and eight I released twelve bass up to four pounds.

CHAPTER EIGHT

Lessons from the Shore

We asked for signs, the signs were sent

It doesn't matter how much you fish for bass, the contrary devils are always going to be as mysterious as Schrödinger's cat, Macavity the cat, the College of Cardinals, the dark lady of the sonnets, the missing Gram Parsons concert tapes, super-string theory, and the Duckworth-Lewis method all rolled into one. How often have you tried in ideal conditions and done poorly, or had a couple of half-hearted chucks on a no-hoper day and caught a few good ones? When you think of all the variables you realise nobody's ever going to work it out completely: size of tide, state of tide, location, distance from shore, water temperature, water clarity, air temperature, wind speed, wind direction, sea-state, bait or fly or lure, time of day, time of year, lunar phase, barometric pressure, colour of underpants … the list goes on forever. If you really can predict what the fish are going to do, I'd like to borrow your forecasting model – or your tea leaves and your crystal ball – for a bash at next year's Grand National. And I think that's why bass are such fun, you're always learning something new and surprising.

- I caught my first double-figure bass a long time ago. I was just a youngster, and one of the old salts weighed it at eleven-and-a-quarter pounds and told me it was the fish of a lifetime. I carried it home bursting with pride. 'Eleven-and-a-quarter pounds,' I announced. 'You should have caught two smaller fish,' said Mother, whose language was of the old school, 'that one's going to be a bastard to get into the deep-freeze.' A prophet is not without honour and all that. By the way it was on half a mackerel after a late summer storm.

For myself I learn a lot by getting out there and trying things. I learn a lot by pondering: if I'm catching fish what am I doing right, and if I'm not what am I doing wrong? But I learn even more by chatting with other folk and observing them, on the shore, in the carpark, the on-line forum, the tackle-shop. (And a side-comment, physical tackle-shops are a great asset, fresh bait and fresh fish-gossip. You may save a few quid on-line, but let's keep real tackle-shops in business. It's worth spending a wee bit more for access to the grapevine.)

Anyway I've realised that almost anyone I meet can offer me a new insight, and a lot of my success is because I'm so happy to snaffle people's tips. You might think sixty-ish years of experience should make me an expert, but I hope those years have shown me how much I don't know about bass. So if other folk have ideas, I'd be a total spanner not to try them out. And that's what I'd recommend to any fisher, keep an open mind and pick brains the way the Chancellor of the Exchequer picks taxpayers' pockets.

I was heading back from a summer morning lure trip when I ran into a young chap who was just starting. I'd had a couple of bass, but as the light came up it was all pollack and wrasse. This fellow had a stout beach-caster and a bucket of crabs. 'Wrasse then?' 'Yes,' he told me, 'and hoping for a few bass.' The magic word. I'm sure he didn't expect it – nobody expects it – but the poor lad went through a bit of a Spanish Inquisition. He was chucking a crab right into the wrack with a rotten bottom link. Mostly this caught wrasse, but he'd managed a few bass over the past days. Lure-fishing, I'd always found the arrival of the wrasse meant the bass were finished.

But then I scratched my woolly hat. Maybe the bass were just a bit deeper, down in the channels and the weed. I was out there next morning with some crabs and a drop-shot rig with a ragwormy soft plastic. The crabs were nippy so I sucked my fingers and tied on the drop-shotting set-up. Five wrasse, three bass, then all my leads were gone. Later I learned – from a chap on a forum – how to make expendable weights. You pour concrete into half a loo roll, stick a paper-clip in the top, and allow to set.

We were having what passes for a heatwave in our damp and chilly land, the sea was like a mirror. I'd been picking away at schoolies off the rocks, mostly using small spoons, occasionally a free-lined live blenny or goby. I popped into my local tackle-shop for a few hooks and a yarn, and there was a fellow buying half a dozen soft plastic prawns. Frankly I thought they looked shite – the hooks were arranged so they'd be swimming the wrong way round.

But I asked the chap how they worked and he lit up like a disco-ball in a lightning storm. Under a bubble-float, chuck it out and twitch it. He'd had bass, wrasse, mackerel, garfish, and pollack. So I headed home and tied up a few prawn-flies. Nothing fancy, I'm not much good at tying flies, just a size two hook, a dark palmered body to suggest legs, some deer-hair

whiskers, and a hair-wing. Casting short and swimming them
around the rocks and weed I had five bass and three pollack
in an hour and a half. Nothing of any size, but they were great
fun on the fly rod – and a sight less hard work than chasing
escapologist blennies around in rock-pools.

When I was a youngster I was down on my local beach in
late spring. I'd had a pretty good evening of it, four or five
bass around three pounds apiece, and I was heading home.
There was a fellow at the other end of the sand so I stopped
by to see how he was getting on. The same as myself, a good
basket of eating fish. 'But we should be seeing some big ones, my
handsome,' he was an older gentleman and very much a local,
the sort of chap who wears a woolly hat to bed and keeps half a
pasty in his pocket at all times.

Now in my youth I used to devour the fishing magazines
and I took every word as revealed truth. 'But I thought autumn
was the time for big ones.' 'Spring and autumn.' said the old boy,
'Mid-summer for schoolies, my pet, the big ones are book-ends.'
Since then whenever there's been a blow in the early season I've
headed out with my trophy baits, squid, razor, half-mackerel;
and I've had as many bass over eight pounds in the early
book-end as in the late one. I think the magazines still say that
November and December are the times for the whoppers, but
my Cornish veteran knew better. And by the way in these parts
it's perfectly OK to be addressed as someone's pet, even if that
someone's a total stranger.

June and we hadn't had a whisper of breeze for a week. I
took my lure tackle for a wander along a white sand beach
on the north coast, not so much fishing with any confidence
as prospecting for new experience. (Experience, as they say, is
what you get when you don't get what you really wanted.) I was
tossing out a sandeel shad, bouncing it through the ripple. I had
a schoolie and a missed pull. Then I tried a baited spoon with a

thin strip of mackerel belly. That delivered a baby flounder.

I was about to knock off when I ran into a lad who was hurling a lure miles into the shallows, dragging it in with a healthy bend in his rod. He was fishing a forty gramme wedge, hauling it in along the bottom. While I watched he had a bass, maybe forty-five centimetres, and a turbot the size of a diet-doctor's digestive biscuit. 'It kicks up such a lot of sand,' he told me, 'the lure could be anything.' It's a method I've used a few times since with decent results. The only change I've made is to swap the treble hook on the wedge for a big single. That way the lure still casts easily and makes a stir-up like an immersion blender in overdrive, but it doesn't get stuck as hard to the sea floor. And it's easier to release fish as well.

- I know I'm not alone on this, but whenever I see 'sea bass' on a menu I want to collar the chef and explain that the UK doesn't have any freshwater bass.

Early September with a moderate breeze out of the north-west, so I headed to the north coast and found the kind of wave that makes a bass fisher's heart sing like a male-voice choir in a brewery, four rows of breakers tumbling across the white sand. Now this is a beach where I'd give you a fiver for every lugworm you could dig, there just aren't any. So I lobbed out a big sandeel. My second cast came up with a bass of a couple of pounds, then no joy. A bunch of ragworms produced as much excitement as a meeting of the parish council rubbish bin sub-committee.

I set out for a wander and I noticed a crunching sound. On with the pocket torch, the sand was carpeted with pale orangey-brown sand-hoppers about half-an-inch long. I wondered how many dozen of the little chaps it would take to fill up a size 4/0 hook. Then I came across a fellow gutting his catch, three fair bass. 'Good on you,' I said, 'what bait are you on?' 'Lug. I had a whole bunch. Fished last night, not a nibble. So I came down again to use them up. Bang, bang, it hasn't stopped.' We looked at the stomach contents of a chubby three-and-a-half pounder: rammed with sand-hoppers. As luck would have it I had some lug in my bag – Boy Scout bass training: be prepared with spare bait – so I tossed a bunch out. As they settled I was into a four pounder. That packet of tired lugworms gave me five chunky fish. No idea why, but I've found bass feeding on sand-hoppers can be horribly fussy about ragworm, sandeel, mackerel, razor clam, mussel, crab, or squid; but they find lugworm hard to resist.

I was spinning from a beach in late spring. It's a spot that shelves steeply at high water, and a Toby or a flying condom can deliver quite a mixed bag: bass, mackerel, mullet, seatrout, flounder. As the light came up I saw a skin-diver flippering his way out beyond the waves. No spear-fishing kit, just a snorkel and a camera. I watched him paddling around and saw he was close to a dimpled patch of water – likely a big shoal of mullet. In he came and he stopped for a quick natter. 'Plenty of bass out there, thirty metres or so.'

Now like a lot of fishers I've often been sent on the wild mullet chase, but this fellow seemed as if he might know his bass from his elbow. 'Any mullet?' 'Yes, tons of them. Then the bass are lying just below the shoals of mullet.' I took off the flying condom and replaced it with a hefty black backed sandeel shad. An almighty heave to get it out beyond the rippled area and I let it drop to the bottom. Then a sink-and-draw retrieve so the shad would be swinging up and down underneath the mullet.

Thump, a three-and-a-half pounder. Since then I must have had a dozen bass from under mullet shoals, and they've all been reasonable fish.

- Our fish-eating habits have changed over the years. When I was young Cornish Sardine was known as pilchard and most of it went to Spain and Italy packed in salt. Plenty of the old lobstermen used bass as pot-bait, and pollack (briefly re-named colin, so red-faced shoppers wouldn't have to ask for a pair of pollacks) was a throw-back. Even monkfish didn't make any money until some canny type started chopping it up with a small biscuit cutter. The little bits of monk became Newlyn Bay Scallops. We ate dogfish a lot, mostly from the chipper. In the south it was called Rock Salmon and in the north Scotch Holibut. (I'm not sure how holibut was spelled, but it was a made-up word anyway, to suggest something a bit like halibut.) There was a market for congers as well, the fish-paste factory.

It was a mid-summer morning about an hour before the dawn, I was chucking a bunch of lugworms from a shingle bank onto an enormous worm-bed. The wave wasn't as big as I might have wished, and the fishing was as lively as a teetotal funeral home in Lent. Then I noticed a boat, maybe a fifteen footer, puttering along the shoreline. At first I thought the son-of-a-gun might be running a seine net along the beach, but I saw in his light that he had a pair of outrigger poles. Right in front of me he slowed the engine and hauled in a good sized bass. Now commercial fishers don't seem to have been bitten by the bug that makes people spend twenty-odd quid on a four inch piece of artfully coloured Japanese plastic, and I've never known them to troll anything but a sandeel-type lure, usually the Eddystone ones. So I dug out a packet of frozen eels and thawed them in the shallows. Chuck one out, twitch it back along the bottom, and that was the ticket, three bass before the sun was up.

• I was fishing plugs in a gentle two foot surf. At first light half a dozen dolphins swam along the shore. In front of me they took it in turns to rip through a wave, do a three hundred and sixty degree somersault, and re-enter the water tail first. There were two fishers at the other end of the strand and I wished they could watch the show, but they were out of hailing range. Then the dolphins headed along the beach again. Right in front of the other chaps they stopped and ran through an encore of the whole acrobatic routine. So why do dolphins do tricks? I'm convinced it's because they're the most dreadful show-offs.

I was lure-fishing from a rocky outcrop but the sea was as flat as a weight-watcher's poppadum under a road-roller. I put on a self-cocking float and set about trying to catch a live-bait. After ten minutes I managed a prawn, very swiftly munched by a half pound wrasse. Back onto my hands and knees, another ten minutes, a three inch blenny, chomped by a baby school-bass.

Then a lad with a bucket came along, and the bucket was heaving with life: shrimps, prawns, gobies, blennies, you name it. He had an aquarium at home and he was stocking it. I didn't think he'd be keen to sell me a few of his new pets as live-bait, but I asked him how he'd managed to catch such a lot. He reached into his pack and showed me a beer bottle with the bottom knocked out. 'Easy. Stick a few bits of limpet in the bottle, sink it in a pool, come back in ten minutes.' Some of the fishing catalogues sell bait traps for twenty or thirty quid, but this lad's home-made effort seems to work just as well. And all you have to do is drink a bottle of beer.

- Anything you eat in the fresh air counts as health-food.

After a slow morning I came home with a three pound bass. When I cleaned it I found nothing but little flounders in its stomach. At the time a couple of my beaches were thick with baby flounders, like chip packets on a Saturday night pavement, and I wondered whether a live one might be a good bass bait. The problem was that the flounder would lie doggo, even bury itself in the sand. Anyway I posted my idea on a forum, and someone suggested a float or a few floaty-beads. I haven't tried the floaty-beads, but an old-fashioned pike bung works a treat, keeping the bait in mid-water.

12lbs exactly, caught in November. We'd had two weeks of southerly and westerly gales, and a lot of fishers were battling with mats of weed. I fished a shallow beach with the wind blowing straight onshore. Lots of wrack on the sand, but I was lobbing my bait into weed-free water eighteen inches deep. The surf was like the inside of a kitchen blender, so I used a 40lb monofilament rig with a twelve inch hook-length.

I had a couple of bass to about 4lbs on razor clam. Then I switched to a whole unwashed squid, my other favoured bait in coloured water.

Einstein was right: if you want a different result it's insanity to keep doing the same thing.

If you're not willing to experiment you can't expect better returns to your fishing trips.

- When I was a youngster I don't remember anyone using elastic thread. I secured my monster baits – typically mackerel sides – with waxed dental floss. I just read some research from one of the big dentistry schools: flossing your teeth has no impact on long-term oral health. So I was right all along, floss belongs in your fishing jacket, not your spongebag.

- Surfers are considerate types, I find, keeping well away from fishers. But there's one in every crowd, the numbskull who follows you along the shore and rides across your line again and again. Why? I used to think these oafs wanted to be in my line-of-sight, so I could admire their fitness and superlative surfing skills. But they tend to be flabby lumps who fall off a lot. So the mystery remains. Likely it's some obscure manifestation of Murphy's Law.

- Someone offered me a vegetarian pasty. That's a contradiction in terms, like government ethics, business English, or Fox News. A pasty's made with skirt of beef, onion, swede, and potato. Any variation means you're eating something that conceivably might be tasty and nutritious, but it isn't a pasty.

CHAPTER NINE

Why People Blank

When every sunrise I see takes the piss out of me

I've learned a lot from people giving me new ideas. I've picked up useful intelligence also from fishers who weren't catching anything, especially if I managed to help them find a bass or two. And I've seen a waterlogged waderful of reasons for those outings with no return. Of course avoiding these traps doesn't guarantee you'll never blank again. There are days when everything seems perfect – the wave, the time, the bait or fly or lure, the old magic trousers – and the fisher's in sparkling form. But things don't always work out, that's Murphy's Law Light. One reason it's called going fishing, not going catching, is the hand of chance. Napoleon liked his generals to be lucky, and there's a random element in a bass trip as well. There's not much to be done about that, but if you steer clear of the commonest acts of fishing folly, I hope most of your trips will be productive.

- I was on a moonlit beach when I saw a young seal in front of me. I moved along the sand, he came too. Fishing was a waste of time, he'd grab anything I caught, and I might snag him as well. So how to make a friendly cub move? I modified the Rolling Stones as I pondered: 'Hey-hey, you-you, get out of my wave' (Get off of my cloud, Decca Records, 1965). I chucked him a squid: big swirl. And there was the plan: I laid a trail of squid up the beach and I caught the odd bass while my chum sat on the sand eating treats. After the squid I threw him sandeels, halving them to make them go further. I hoped he'd stick around to surprise the dog-walkers, my Cornish underwater wrasse-hound. But such luck, he ducked back into the drink at first light.

Fishing at the wrong time

A lot of the bass fishers I meet are heading in the opposite direction. On beaches they're toddling up from the strand as I'm clambering into my waders, on fly and lure marks I'm going home as they're arriving. They might be missing a trick. Bass feed mostly in darkness, while the morning lure-jockeys are still duvet-bound. And I'm convinced they feed hardest at the end of the night, when the late evening bait-chuckers are snuggled up in pyjamas, cuddling their nightcap Ovaltines and whiskies (in separate vessels I trust). At dusk the fish seem to take their time. Towards dawn they're in the last chance saloon, stoke up now before the noisy beach-goers pitch up and the nocturnal creatures vanish. Or maybe they think breakfast is the most important meal of the day, who knows? As long as it works, who cares?

I wouldn't wish my own bad sleeping habits on anyone – I'm incapable of lying down for more than five hours at a stretch – but most folk don't go bass fishing as often as I do. So if you're blanking too much, give it a bash: try hauling yourself from your cosy pit at stupid o'clock, see what happens.

Shuffling along with the lost

In summer I run into plenty of holiday-makers looking for bass on the rocks and the beaches. There's one thing I notice often. I'll be fishing when I see a headlamp heading for the water's edge. Ten minutes later another fisher arrives and goes to the same spot as the first. Then another, and another. They don't crowd me because I'm invisible, no headlamp, but they clump together like electoral candidates round a baby or flies on a cowpat.

At an unfamiliar spot it's tempting to assume that other folk have inside track, to follow the crowd. But it's a rotten idea. Much better to make your own decision where to try that first cast. Even if there is a guaranteed bass-magnet position, the tag-along fisher won't be in it but right beside it, just close enough to watch the first bod catch all the fish – and that's no fun at all. More likely you're traipsing along behind someone who showed up first but who's every bit as clueless as you are.

I know my areas inside out, mostly because they're so few, and people ask me which is the better end of a beach or which little cove's my favourite. They never get a straight answer, they get the old politician's answer: it depends. And it does, on the size of the wave, the time of year, the state of the tide, how much sand was shifted by the last storm, and so ad infinitum. Very small variations in conditions can make a huge difference to the bass.

One of my old reliable beach areas was a desert for a year because half an inch of dredging spoil overlaid the lugworm beds. A productive rock mark died the death when a wrack clump the size of a single bed was torn away by a storm. Things change. So don't follow along like a sheep. That first lamp, the bellwether for the whole flock, probably belonged to a fisher who had a few good bass from the magic spot – five years ago, in different weather, when the shore-line had a different shape, and at a different time of the season.

I was on a north coast beach in late October. There was a brisk northerly breeze and the wave was pushing along the strand. At half tide there's a gully ten yards out from the west end of the sand, so that's where I started. Sure enough plenty of bass to sandeels, and at first light I saw clouds of the little chaps being swept through the gully by the flow, like grubby snowflakes in an inner city blizzard. Two days later I was on the same beach, but the wind was light from the east. Not much wave so I hiked to the flattest, most exposed area. A bunch of ragworms, a little weight, a short cast, and a few twitches to keep the bait on the move: two decent bass, 60cm and 55cm. On the way back to the car I met three chaps fishing the gully – blanking and decidedly disgruntled. 'We thought this must be jack-spot,' one told me with the outraged incredulity of a tax auditor hearing that the receipts vanished in a freak tornado, 'I saw you here the other day, your rod was never straight.'

Locking into a master-plan

There are lots of reasons I fish by myself and one's adaptability. Generally at bed-time I've decided where to go next morning. But sometimes I wake up, poke my head out of the door, and find our promised moderate westerly's morphed into a southerly gale, which makes a complete mockery of my original plan. No problem, I just grab different gear or different bait, Bob's your uncle. I won't have a fishing partner waiting forlorn in the wrong carpark or showing up with beach tackle when I've decided to chuck a fly into a sea-pool.

Now I'm not recommending that everyone fish alone. For a lot of fishers the craic is a good deal of the pleasure; and if you go to even marginally risky spots, having some company's a no-brainer. What I would say is that you're better off with a Plan A – four o'clock behind the pub – and a few back-ups, Plans B through D, just in case conditions don't turn out as expected. Fishing in the surf might have been an excellent notion yesterday evening. If it looks like a dreadful mistake when morning comes around, go somewhere else. 'It seemed like a good idea at the time,' is a pretty thick excuse for a muck-up. 'It seemed like a good idea twelve hours ago,' is as thick as two short planks.

- Fishers complain that the government ignores us. No big surprise, the last prime minister I remember fishing was Sir Alec Douglas-Home (1963-1964). He didn't chase bass, just salmon in the Tweed. And he didn't last long in office either. Maybe Westminster doesn't get along with fishers.

Eyes wide shut

Fishing isn't just about catching fish, it's also about watching the wave. Time by the water beats the wetsuit pants off the natural history programmes on the television, so I doze through them and conserve energy for my early morning outings. As the light comes up I see sharks, dolphins surfing the breakers, seals scoffing rays, mullet and seatrout leaping, sandeels dimpling, whitebait flipping, cormorants duck-diving, terns and gannets crashing into baitfish, bass swirling and boiling. (Once in a while I see skinny-dippers as well, but their appearances are uncommon and very unpredictable.)

When I mention my sightings to other fishers, often they've noticed nothing. Why? Because they've been staring fixedly at a rod-tip, willing it to thump; or gazing at a popper or the end of a fly-line, lost in admiration for its seductive progress through the fizz. These folk aren't just missing out on free entertainment, they're missing out on fish as well. Seals give you a pointer on how far to cast, diving birds show you exactly where to cast, scattering baitfish help you

133

choose your fly or lure, surface-feeding bass must be telling you something worth knowing, and naked bathers always raise a smile. So if you're struggling for bites, try scanning the water. Hold your surf rod so you don't need to peer at the tip, let your lure or fly take care of itself, and use your eyes to find the fish.

Fishing too far out

I love it when I can help other fishers turn a poor outing into a success, and often I only have to convince them to cast shorter. It's easy to look at the wave and persuade yourself the feeding zone will be outside the wild water; or to feel an almighty fling's the only way to justify the six hundred quid you spent on your new beach-casting outfit; or just to enjoy the buzz of double-hauling a Gummy Sandeel half way across the ocean. And it must work somewhere. But on my marks the action's close in, in the shallow froth that looks like an aerobics class in a bubble-bath.

If you're not sure how close is too close, try a long cast, then bring your bait back towards the shore a few yards every few minutes. With lures and flies the humungous hurl's less of a problem, even the longest chuck winds up closer in as you retrieve. But I fare best when I don't waste time plumbing the barren depths; so I cast directly to the bass-lies, or at a fairly tight angle to the shore. And I always fish all the way in, until the swivel or the line-loop's almost hitting the end-ring.

Late September and the surf was small, less than three feet. There was a full moon and I could see another figure along the sand. A proper bass fisher, holding the rod, lamp away from the water, this chap had read the rule-book. I had two decent bass in my first three chucks so I switched to a half mackerel to see about a bigger fish. Then the stranger came along. He'd been at it since sundown, two flounders. He watched me toss my bait into the foam. 'Is that as far as you cast?' 'It is today.' 'Any good?'

he asked, 'Or maybe that's a silly question, you just arrived, right?' 'Yes, but I've had a couple.' 'OK, I've been dropping in the last breaker. I guess I might as well try your method. Here goes nothing,' he said lobbing gently. A few minutes later, 'Holy guacamole, a bite.' My half-mackerel didn't produce any monsters, but that was a super trip. My new pal beached three bass, the first he'd ever caught in four trips to Cornwall. And I learned a bizarre expression of surprise. I don't use it, but expressions are like boot-socks, you can't have too many.

Rainwater run-off

Here's a really annoying bit of outdoorsy folk wisdom: 'There's no such thing as bad weather, just the wrong clothes.' Excuse me, but that's tosh. What about a lightning storm, what d'you wear to stop yourself being fried? Or a howling gale with hailstones like golf balls, let's see how the Goretex undies handle that one.

And there's one weather event that can play merry hell with the bass in some places: persistent rain. A few of my surf and rock fishing spots are sinks for a lot of rainwater sources. One beach sits at the bottom of a funnel-shaped valley, so all the precipitation from several square miles flows into the surf. A rocky cove I fish is similar, just on a much smaller scale. And another beach is studded with drainpipes that carry filthy surface-water from the roads and carparks straight into my fishing wave.

In winter a lot of really wet weather wrecks these spots. Winter rainfall's cold to begin with, then it runs to the sea across chilly fields and lanes, becoming even icier and dirtier on the way; and I find the bass just vanish out into the deeper, warmer water which is unaffected by the frigid, muddy gunk. So in nippy conditions I avoid these spots after a downpour, heading instead for a mark where less run-off ends up in the ocean.

In summer the rain isn't too cool, but it still makes the waves pretty grubby. Bass seem to be OK with very coloured water – folk catch them in the upper Bristol Channel after all – but they can't feed by sight when the sea's like Brown Windsor soup. So in a Cornish monsoon I leave my lure and fly kit in the garage, my ragworms and sandeels in the fridge. For my money, turbid surf calls for baits with scent and juice, so I use lugworms, razor clams, mussels, blood-and-gutsy mackerel heads, or my favourite – big unwashed squid.

Putting down roots

Some of my areas have detailed reputations: fish the gully by the pasty-shaped point, head for the west end of the beach. On the rare occasion I run into someone, it will be at one of these reputed hot-spots, and that's where the fisher will stay, flogging the water relentlessly with a succession of lures or flies, or waiting patiently for the bait to be picked up by a head-thumping whopper. If no bass oblige, it's back to the car. 'Nothing doing today.' Which statement is half-true. 'Nothing doing today in that precise bit of water,' that's the real John Dory.

So if you're blanking – even in your magic mark – try a little wander. The bass have to be somewhere; and if they aren't here, that leaves somewhere else as the only logical option. I believe twenty-odd minutes is long enough in any spot. If it doesn't deliver, move on and maybe come back later. Ronald Reagan famously told his staff, 'Don't do something, just stand there.' Great advice for politicians, whose efforts usually make the situation even more stuffed up than it was to begin with. But just standing there isn't always the way to catch bass.

I fished a little inlet, shallow and weedy, and the action was non-stop. A small surface lure brought me a good bass for the kitchen, then I switched to a weedless soft plastic so I could release the rest of my fish easily. Next morning conditions were much the same, so back to the inlet; where I had a micro-pollack off the top and mini-wrasse on the softie. 'Maybe I just need to wait for the tide to make a bit more,' I thought. But I have a proper bass fisher's attention span, a little shorter than that of a multi-tasking gnat. So in the meantime I beetled off quarter of a mile to the west and had a try in a channel between two reefs. Six casts, three fish, and a really good one that came off.

Another way fishers anchor themselves is literally by using an anchor, a lead that grips the bottom. I know a wired lead makes for an easy life. You can rest the rod, slump onto a kit-box, nibble a wormy sandwich, have a cuppa, or (and I've seen this more than once) check Facebook and Twitter on your mobile telephone. But you can do all those things in a toxic cafeteria at a motorway service station – with slime-free sandwiches no less – so why waste beach time on them? You fish a lot more effectively with a bomb weight; then your tackle wanders through the surf, stopping in the bassy depressions in the sand. And if the sea's too gentle to shift your gear, twitch the sinker along the bottom. Move it a few feet, let it sit a while, repeat the dose.

• I spent a few years in Botswana. The country has no coastline, so the language has no vocabulary to describe seafood. When people started importing frozen prawns from Mozambique, the prawn was named after the local land creature it most resembled, the cockroach. Luckily restaurant menus tended to be written in English, so we never had to order piri-piri cockroaches.

Miniature baits and hooks

Tiny baits don't lead to blanks, just tiny fish. Sure, once in a while you'll see some jammy bod in a magazine with a giant bass that took a single harbour ragworm on a size 6 hook. Once in a while a government minister gives a straight answer to a tough question. Longshots occasionally come up. But hefty bass need lots of calories, and for a good chance of a decent fish you're better offering something worth eating – not an appetiser, but a main meal for a hearty appetite. A chunky bunch of worms is the smallest I'll ever use. More often it's a plump crab or squid, a giant sandeel, or a meaty portion of mackerel, mussel, or razor clam. And big hooks, 3/0s and up, are the best way I know to avoid bait-swallowing tiddlers; and to be reasonably sure of a secure hook-hold in that long-awaited whopper.

Bait in the water at all times

When bass start to show on a lure-fishing spot – swirling behind the plug or fly, slashing at baitfish – it's natural to want to put your gear in front of them. If I were to spot a fisher sitting motionless on a rock while the surface is a boiling feeding frenzy, I'd check for vital signs.

Of course we should be casting into the action. But I see wildly animated types lashing the water half to death with the same lure or fly over and over again, and that makes no sense at all. When you've brought your Sammy or your Bucktail Deceiver through the zone a fair few times untouched, and varied your retrieve speed from dead slow to demented, it's time to face facts: whatever the bass are eating it doesn't look like a Sammy or a Deceiver.

It's hard to stop casting when the surface is alive with fish, but the time it takes to clip on a different lure or tie on a new fly is time very well spent.

Bait-fishers sometimes drive up the same psychological dead-end, you've got to be in it to win it. So out go some fat lugworms. And out they stay, and stay, and stay. The fisher just can't reel in, a big bass might be inches away, leave it five more minutes. And when finally the bait's checked it turns out to be empty worm-skins wrapped in an impenetrable coating of fine weed.

You can't catch fish when your gear's on dry land, that much is true. But you won't do much good with the wrong fly or lure, or with a bait that's long past its take-by date.

• The metric system's OK, but who's going to brag about a 4.545 kilogram-er?

Away in a private bubble

I sometimes see another fisher catching nothing while I'm doing well. I'd expect a polite visit and a few questions about the bait or lure or fly I'm using, or how far I'm casting; at least a casual natter and a careful sideways squizz at the end of my line. It's amazing how rarely that happens – until I wander along and start the conversation. A lot of people seem to think they have to work it all out for themselves, that successful bass fishers are grumpy, secretive miseries who wouldn't tell you the time of day.

And fair enough, I can be grumpy if some chatterbox stands beside me endlessly, my peace and quiet shattered by a non-stop eruption of blether about overpaid football stars or overpriced mobile telephones. I can be secretive too. When I find a few big bass I don't tell anyone where I've been fishing because I don't want my marks over-run or gill-netted. But if we're both at the same spot and all someone wants is an update on what's working, I'm a sweetheart. Not only will I tell you the lure that's doing the trick, I'll give you one as well – as long as there's a spare in my bag. And I find most of my fellow-fishers are no different.

So don't be shy. If the fish aren't obliging, see if anyone else is faring any better, find out what's hitting the spot for the other folk on the shore. Some will tell you their life stories ('Father used to fish out of Penzance…') and some will be curt ('Razor clam, second wave'), but most will steer you right – if only you ask. And return the favour.

When you're doing well, encourage the blankers to pick your brain, give them a helping hand or a helping squid or some helping lugworms. Apart from match-fishing – which I would try only if the alternative were to be drowned slowly in ice-cold pig-slurry – ours is a collaborative sport. It's fishers united against the contrariness and unpredictability of the bass. Don't feel you need to go it alone.

Late October, we'd had days of light easterlies so there was no surf anywhere. I was on the beach at four. Another fellow had been there all night for two flounders. I used a one ounce weight with a bunch of ragworms – ten or so on a 4/0 – casting twenty-odd yards and twitching the bait in. Two schoolies and one a few whiskers shy of 10lbs. (Five ounces of whiskers to be picky.) The other chap tried my dodge and managed a five-pounder.

You can't change the conditions, but you can change the way you fish. And when bass are hard to find, a moving bait or a lure can be a good way to search the water. A bit more effort than hurling out a grip-lead and lounging in a camp-chair, but often it's much more productive.

Asleep at the wheel

Non-fishers love to laugh at our yarns about the one that got away. They must reckon we stand around by the water puffing on gigantic spliffs, then imagine bites from even more gigantic fish. But a lot of lost bass are real, and often they escaped because they took when least expected. I ran into pair of beach-fishers with one of those tales that make you laugh and cry at the same time.

One chap had been caught short, so he shoved his rod onto a tripod and dropped his waders. Cue a wrenching hit, and the rod flew from the tripod and along the shore. He galloped after it – a good effort considering his legs were tied together with neoprene, and something that must have been fun to watch – and grabbed the handle. But the reel was jammed with sand, so the next strong pull from the fish parted the line.

That one was hearsay, but I've been an eye-witness to similar disasters. Take the holiday-maker I met on a rocky point. He chucked his surface lure a few yards from his boots, then dug out a tobacco tin to roll a smoke. A mighty slurp as a six-pounder seized the plug, then an almost inaudible ping and an extremely audible bellow when his fluorocarbon leader popped. Then there was a fly-fisher who tucked his rod under his arm while he took a snapshot of the sunrise. You can guess what happened next, an explosive boil followed by a single searing yank as a very decent bass swam off with his Clouser Minnow.

So what to do? I don't recommend ignoring or deferring calls of nature for obvious reasons, and depriving ourselves of ciggies, sandwiches, warming cups of tea, or even photo-opportunities would take the fun out of fishing for most of us. What I would say is that lures or flies are best out of the water when you take a break. With a bait in the surf I sometimes keep fishing while taking care of other business – but I'm only going to prop my rod on the sand-spike when the drag's been slackened off all the way.

Tightening at the wrong time

I use that word – tightening – with care for my meaning. If your hooks are sharp, there's no need for a sledgehammer strike. But I see lure-maniacs yanking ferociously at a take, often with unintended consequences, an airborne plug flying at the fisher's head through a tsunami of colourful vocabulary. When a bass hits a lure, the first whack often seems to be with its head, a predator-style Glasgow kiss to disable its prey. Belting the rod back in response just pulls the lure out of the feeding area. It takes self-discipline – and I sometimes stuff it up – but I try not to raise my rod-tip until I feel the solid resistance of a bass with a hook in its mouth.

On the beach I watch folk hoicking their rods back with wild abandon, like caber-tossers warming up for the Highland Games after one too many drams. A waste of effort, a rapid tug tends to be a short tug, often not enough to take up the curve in the line. (Even with braid there can be quite a bow as the wind, wave, and tide tow it along the shore.) Better to wait until there's a hefty feel to the pull, or some slack. Then walk up the beach to drive the hook into your fish.

With a live-bait there nearly always is a killing slash before the bass tries to eat her treat. One big jerk, then nothing – until she comes back to swallow her victim. I like to let the bass swim away with the once-live-bait. As a rule it'll take some line, stop, then move off again. And that second run, that's when I close the bail-arm and hope it's a monster.

Blunt hooks

If your hooks aren't sharp it doesn't matter when or whether you tighten. Dull hook-points wreck your chances of catching bass. And if you lose a decent fish because of shoddy gear, it's entirely your own fault, you've been a perfect twit; so you have every right to howl profanities at the sky and to flagellate yourself with a bunch of lugworms. It may seem like a faff to check or sharpen your hooks all the time, but it's good policy. Much better to sacrifice a few minutes of gear-in-the-water time than to drop a whopper because the cheapest element of your tackle's no good.

- I'm convinced people post on fishing forum sites because their families refuse to listen to yet one more report about the weed, the wave, and the weather. And if you land a good bass – or even lose one – you have to tell someone the whole story, don't you?

Scaring the fish away

I reckon headlamps on the water and leaping about on the shore are good ways to guarantee the bass do a bunk, but I bump into a lot of fishers who don't share my views. I see mobile lighthouses jigging around like a cross between a Maasai wedding party and a boozy barn-dance; then stomping into a small wave and focussing their brilliant beams on the surf. Sometimes they ask me why I think they're not having bites. When I tell them, they say, 'But I've caught bass fishing like this before.' Well, I had a bass two miles up a tiny brook on a pheasant tail nymph in bright sunlight, but I'd be surprised to catch another that way.

Looking for the magic bullet

When something works, common-sense says we ought to keep it in mind. Whether it's a lure or a spot or a bait or whatever, if it does the job it should go into the notebook. But there can be a problem. It wasn't just that lure that delivered, it was that lure fished on a slow retrieve past two wrack clumps at sunset in late June in a Force three west wind at high water on a five metre tide with big sandeels in the fifteen degree Celsius two foot wave, a cyclonic low in sea area Rockall, nineteen degrees air temperature, a waning moon in Aquarius, a cheese sandwich in your pocket, and a total twerp in Ten Downing Street. And fishers often forget the context, concluding simply, 'Magic effing lure.'

Fish the same lure when the whitebait have replaced the sandeels – or when there's ham in the sandwiches and a new twerp in Downing Street – and the magic lure may be tragic.

The same confusion kicks in when the fishing grapevine comes to life. The word's about that some holiday-maker from France had three six pounders from Porth-plonker, which now has a rammed carpark and a heaving mob of hyperventilating fishers – probably doing poorly. Why? Because the French bod was successful a week ago, when the weather was different, the tide was different, the wave was different, and the shore wasn't aglow with headlamps.

Even bait can lead us astray. One of my spots has a healthy razor clam population, and low water lets me drop my gear right in the middle of the beds. I had a few bass and a few giltheads. Then I was in my local tackle-shop stocking up on frozen razors for the next set of tides. Half a dozen summer visitors heard what I'd been catching; and in spite of my two-penny-worth they cleared the deep-freeze. I suspect they didn't fare that well. They were off to fish a muddy stretch of shore, crawling with lugworms, empty of razors.

Now I'm not saying we should ignore success, far from it. What I am saying is that we should be wary of attributing success to one particular cause. A whole raft of factors come together to provide decent fishing: weather, mark, wave, bait, time, tide, lucky bobble-hats. There are so many different bits of context that the human brain can't even identify them all, never mind figure out which make the most difference. The old saying's true, success has many fathers, failure's a bastard. When we take good fish we never know for certain which father to credit. I kept a detailed catch log for a while, but it didn't last: I was spending more time recording twenty-odd observations than I was fishing. And I still didn't know if I was capturing the stuff that's really key. So the best I can do is take everything I know about bass and their often unfathomable ways, then see what feels right for today's conditions.

Early May was chilly and the fish seemed to be moving sluggishly. There were some baby mullet in the coves, and I winkled out the odd bass on a black and silver jointed plug. I met a holiday fisher who was blanking on a Patchinko, so I offered him one of my mullet specials. It caught him his lunch and made his mouth look like one of those yellow smiley faces – the sort that make me want to say, 'Don't tell me what kind of day to have'. Two months later I met the same chap in the same spot, still using the black and silver job. By now the water was toasty, whitebait were sprinkling from the waves, and the fake baby mullet was going down as well as a T-bone steak at a vegan picnic. But once he switched to one of my Tobys he was away to the races.

Some fishers develop an almost mystical attachment to spots, lures, baits, or methods. Or maybe they fall in love. Either way they seem helpless to change what they're doing, even if it's failing horribly. Often I reckon this is because of a single really memorable success; which, defying anything like sound judgment, they put down to the one thing that stuck in their minds.

I was casting to a bed of lugworms, there were plenty of fish. No monsters – I find lugworm beds good for numbers, not for giants. I ran into a fellow using a whole squid which can be a way of sorting out a big bass. We had a chat as he watched his motionless rod – all he'd managed was a dogfish. It wasn't just whole squid, he told me, it was freeze-dried squid, reconstituted in warm pilchard oil, then stuffed with tinned sardines, WD40, and crab-meat. Why? Because his pal had a ten pound bass on this cocktail. 'Wow, here?' I asked him. 'No, from a boat in the Bristol Channel, fishing for winter cod.' I tried to give the man a fistful of lugworms, but he was determined to tough it out with his double-figure bass bait; which might have been a good idea – had we been three months later in the year, in fifty foot deeper water, and a hundred and some miles to the north-east.

Mid-summer and the coves were full of sandeels two to three inches long. Almost any small lure would do the job, but a shad was best, the single hook making it easy to release the bass swiftly. Along came a holiday-maker bristling with expensive kit. His lure struck me as a bit odd: five or six inches long, green and orange. 'It's a beauty,' he told me, 'seven bass in two hours, nothing under five pounds.' 'What, this morning? I thought you'd just arrived.' 'No last year, October, west coast of Ireland.' He'd promptly bought himself a lifetime supply of this gizmo – and I bet it's super when the bass are on pollack or wrasse – and used nothing else. He hadn't had another bass since October either.

Even the way we retrieve our lures can pick up that magical aura which makes it hard to try anything different. With a paddle-tail shad I go for a bit of a stop-start number. Not so much sink-and-draw, more pause-and-crank. I've watched my shads in calm water, and they look very appetising as they flutter briefly before skipping ahead. Appetising to me at least, but what do I know? I like my little fish fried in flour and dunked in garlic mayonnaise with a wedge of lemon. And there are days when the bass are on sandeel and my seductively dancing shad does me no good at all, but when winding the little fellow straight in at a steady, moderate speed has me into a fish on almost every cast.

One last thing that can muck up our chances, too much faith in our theories. We all come up with ideas about bass, from our experience, by reading, when we chat with successful fishers. I have a woolly hatful of views on how to find the fish, and often my notions steer me in the right direction. But they're theories not laws of nature, and they don't apply all the time. For example I believe with a passion that bass feed harder in shallow, stirred-up froth than in the calmer deeps, and hundreds of fishing trips have shown me that this is true.

Except when it isn't. Once in a Norwegian blue moon my short casts have my lure or bait in water that's as dead as a Monty Python parrot, but an almighty heave for the horizon puts me straight into the taking zone. Equally I'm convinced that whitebait call for small lures, and my little Tobys work an absolute treat. Except when they don't, when bass with stomachs jammed with whitebait turn up their noses at anything less than five inches long. Theories work in theory. When they don't work in practice, we need to ignore them, to put them aside and experiment.

- It's funny the way everyone feels they can wander up to a fisher and ask, 'Caught anything?' I mean, we don't stop the dog-walkers and say, 'Had a good run?' or 'Done a poo yet?'

Late summer, warm water, and sandeels flipping at the surface. Tactics were obvious, a three inch plug skimming along the top, a rock solid option in the conditions. Half a dozen casts, some straight to swirling bass, and not so much as a follow, I might as well have been shoving a stiff whisky in front of a rabid teetotaller. A shallow diver, again the right size to suggest the sandeels, just as snootily ignored. Then laziness got the better of me, I was tired of casting and retrieving so I shoved on a pinky-white weedless soft plastic ragwormy effort six inches long. I let it sink to the bottom and gave a tiny tweak. Four decent bass in six casts.

8lbs 5oz, caught on a large bunch of ragworms as an autumn storm was starting to build. A lot of fishers focus on the end of a blow, but I find the start can be even more productive, and often less weedy.

I think of ragworms as a sight-bait so I like them when the water's pretty clear. Heavily coloured surf has me on baits with more juice and scent, such as lugworm, razor clam, mackerel head, or whole unwashed squid.

So here's the nub: if you lock in on one little aspect of your fishing – a time, a place, a bait, a lure, a fly, a retrieve, a way of doing things – and turn it into your lucky charm, the thing you'll never change, you're setting yourself up to fail. There is no magic bullet. What worked a treat yesterday often is a disaster today, what produced monsters at one spot may throw up nothing but tiddlers at another. So if you're not catching decent fish, do something different, almost no matter what. As Sir Thomas Beecham said, 'Try everything once except incest and folk dancing.' (I have no problem with folk dancing, so I'd say 'incest and dynamite.')

- In the UK in 2015 the Met Office started naming storms. In the USA they've had names for their hurricanes for ages; and as in the UK they alternate between a boy's name and a girl's name. More people are injured by hurricanes with female names. When folk hear that Hurricane Derek or Dave is on the way they're nervous and they evacuate. But if it's Hurricane Diane or Dorothy they reckon she'll be a sweet little thing, so they stay put. An exquisite combination of sexism and stupidity.

CHAPTER TEN

Chasing the Big Ones

Four strong winds that blow lonely,
seven seas that run high

West Cornwall has some lovely bass fishing, but it's not held to be much of an area for really big fish. The NFSA publishes specimen weights for shore-caught bass. In Cornwall the target's eight pounds, for Channel Island fishers it's nine pounds, and it's nine-and-a-half for the bods in Dorset. So I seem to live in tiddler country where only the pasties are giants. But I manage my share of large fish. In the last two seasons I've caught twenty-nine between seven and nine pounds, five between nine and ten, and four of the fabled double-figure jobs. Whoppers always are a bit hit-and-miss, there just aren't that many about, but there are common threads running through most of my biggest catches. So if you dream of that elusive ten-pounder – and a lot of people tell me they do, especially on slow days at work – here are my ideas about how to find her.

Some fishers are plain lucky, but not a lot

We've all heard tales of improbable monsters. What about the holiday-maker chucking feathers from a pier at lunch-time only to land a nine pound bass, or the flounder-fisher who fluked a club record on a baited spoon with a size 6 hook? I find these stories rather annoying. No, I find them utterly infuriating. Someone who would have been pleased with a few mackerel for supper or with a fatty-flattie is holding what a true bass fisher would see as the catch of a life-time, it seems like a dreadful waste – pearls before jammy punters. But here's the good news, it doesn't happen very often. Most real trophies are taken by fishers out at night aiming specifically for big bass – not just bass, big bass.

- When I use a bait that needs elastic thread I lay it on the seat of my little backpack-stool. The fabric's black, it gives me a good background to see what I'm doing. And there's a spin-off benefit, on foggy nights it's easy to find my kit. I just take a deep breath, then follow my nose towards the smell of manky mackerel, stale squid, and rotten razor.

Wild and woolly weather

Nearly all my fat-ladies have been late in spring or in the winter months. April and May have done me well and so has the slot from November to January. This may have to do with migration patterns, but I think it's down to the state of the sea, not too cold and often wild. As we tell the holiday-makers – and it's not a total porkie – summer can give us settled weather, soft breezes. Pleasant for wandering the coves with a fly-rod or a lure outfit, and it's lots of fun to catch bass on light tackle. But even if I cast only to the biggest swirls I mostly find schoolies. They're so fast to hit a fly or a lure that the better fish never seem to get a look-in. In shallow still water I sometimes see little pods of bass, a few fish cruising along together. Toss a fly or a bait in front of them and Murphy's Law kicks straight in, it's always one of the nippers that's quickest to peel off and grab it.

I land my big lumps when the rocks are being smashed by walloping Atlantic swells, the beaches are endless vistas of white water, and the dog-walkers' jackets are flapping like maiden aunts at an orgy. My theory's that truly hairy surf puts the babies off, but the lunkers love a crashing wave and all the bass treats it washes in; and with no competition from schoolies they find my bait.

And that's the trick, I'd say, fishing in conditions the big bass appreciate, lots of easy food, but avoiding the tinkers. I might have more trophies on the fly or on a lure if I were prepared to wander the headlands in the sort of gale that clears out the tiddlers. But I'm not. I don't mind being sleep-deprived, chilly, wet, or windblown for my sport, but I draw the line at being drowned. So my whopper-hunting's from safe sand, and that means bait-fishing gear. In too many years to contemplate I've only ever taken two big bass on lures, one on the fly. All three were in millpond conditions, all were very nearly unrepeatable strokes of luck: I saw the fish lurking in the margins and cast to them – and that's not going to happen very often, even if you fish as much as I do.

I know a lot of fishers do well with a big live-bait fished close in on a calm night. It's a tactic I've tried a fair amount, whenever I catch something I can fish live, and it's produced quite a lot of bass – but never a really big one. I reckon a wriggling whiting, mackerel, pollack, or pout is the predator equivalent of a warm bacon sandwich with melting butter and a lovely runny egg, so irresistible that it's grabbed by the first bass that finds it; and in still water that's much more likely to be a five-pounder than a ten-pounder.

In a small wave or a flat sea I've fared a bit better with a hefty free-lined dead-bait, usually one or two whole squid or the front half of a decently-sized mackerel with a dollop of dangling guts. This has caught me a few six-to-eight pounders, generally from within three or four yards of the shore. When there's not much fizz I stand – or better sit – well back from the water's edge to lob my bait; and I keep as still as bank holiday traffic on the A30 – big bass are easy to scare off, even when it's as dark as a bag. But no matter how carefully I fish the gentler conditions, I still catch a lot more small and medium-sized fish than legitimate brutes. Quite simply there are more of them to be had, and the most humungous bait never seems to be too big for a very average-sized bass. So for the best chance of monsters I'd rather stick to fishing the wild whistling westerlies, the waves that bash around too much for the littler ones.

Early November, the first real autumn blow was brewing out of the southwest, gusts to forty-five knots. I headed for a flat beach with the wind onshore. Parking the car I ran into a fellow who was leaving. 'Unfishable,' he told me, 'I'm going to try in the shelter of the headland.' The surf was churning and it was going to take a wired lead to keep my gear in the water, but I thought it looked promising. I tied a couple of plump razor clams onto a pair of 4/0s and planted my boots at the edge of the wave.

A gust subsided, and I lobbed fifteen yards into the froth; then toddled up the sand and turned my back to the weather as the backwash yanked at my braid like a juvenile delinquent mastiff at its lead. In about five minutes I felt a thump, then a smidgen of slack line, maybe half a yard.

I walked up the beach to tighten and after a head-shaking, zig-zagging fight I had a nine-and-a-half pounder at my feet. I could see squalls in the distance, a flash of sheet lightning, so just one more chuck. A seven-ish pounder which I released. But returning the fish through the wave gave me cold wet hands – up to my armpits – so I headed home for a cockle-warming coffee.

152

Bigger tides bring bigger fish

I don't think it's quite as important as the weather, but three quarters of my trophy bass have come on decent-sized tides. In Mount's Bay the smallest neaps generally run just under four metres above datum, the springs between five-and-a-half and six and a bit. I've had most of my best fish on tides in excess of five metres. I reckon stronger tidal flows stir up more bass treats; and when the breeze is onshore and stiff, these treats concentrate in the shallows, a munchie fantasy for predators large enough to deal with the hairy conditions. That said I'll still go out with my whopper baits in a good storm even if the tide's a tiddler, and I've taken fish in the six to nine pound range on wee small neaps, but not nearly as many as on the springs. I hate to rub it in like dubbin, but if your fishing time's limited – unlike mine – and you can't ditch your work or family commitments, you're best advised to focus on the bigger tides.

• Ragworms are a bit like strips of cloth, but lugworms bear no resemblance to any ear I've ever seen. They don't look like big bolts either. A total mystery.

Learn to love your alarm-clock

Some experts say you can catch big bass in daylight, especially if the sky's grey and the surf's crashing. I'm sure they're right, but I've never had much joy after sunrise, schoolies for sure, but nothing worth weighing. Black night's good, but the best time of all – at least according to my records – is when the first weak gleam of dawn's showing in the east. Of course a lot of fishing success is down to a self-fulfilling prophecy, and when I see that pale glow in the sky I half-expect a good take. So often that's when I check my hooks, refresh my bait, and adjust my lucky hat – and I always have more bites when my headgear's at the right rakish angle. Still

I'm convinced your best chance of a bragging bass comes at times when most fishers are snuggled up in their duvets for that last sweet snooze, hoping their partners will get up and put the kettle on.

Cast short, fish the shallows

I'm always a believer in fishing close in and shallow, often a good deal closer and shallower than most. For big fish I'm not so much a believer, more a wild-eyed raving fanatic. It's only a rule of thumb – a thumb that's well scarred from hooks, gill plates, and spikey fins, it should be said – but I find that too many small bass mean I'm casting too far. In rough weather the giants are much nearer in than the average specimens. In fact I can't recall a single bass over eight pounds that took at a range greater than twenty yards from my boots; and in a screaming sea I never wade deeper than my ankles. That's when a scary swell rolls in, so my feet are dry as a bone when the wave's out.

Between eighteen inches and three feet seems to be the magic depth, right in the wildest froth, where the surface looks like the top of a pint of stout and the undertow jerks at the line like a tug-of-war team in a filthy mood. I think the big fish are strong enough to deal with brutal turbulence, to just wash around in it, their bulkiness keeping them from being smacked into the bottom or swept onto dry land. Meanwhile the schoolies play safe in the deeper, less churned-up areas, even though the food's much more concentrated closer in, especially in a spell of properly demented weather.

Here's another advantage of fishing the shallows. In a big blow a steep strand produces a mean, sucking dump. Flatter sand gives me a lot of smaller, bubblier waves, up to a dozen. This makes life much easier. The weight isn't yanked from the bottom, I don't need to shuffle up and down like a high energy line-dancer to absorb the tugging of the sea. And I can feel the bites even if they're gentle – a whopper often takes as softly as a mini-rockling with toothache.

But there's one problem with a big fish sea. In a total howler – when it's difficult to stand up or to cast even fifteen yards into the gale, when my backpack gallops up the shore, when I'm afraid my woolly hat's going to wind up in East Anglia – the swirly surf sometimes leads to a lot of fankled leaders. This happens most with well-sized baits like a whole squid or half a mackerel, which can behave like exuberant merry-go-round horses in a mosh-pit. A really short hook-length, down to eighteen or even twelve inches, helps combat this; and I often use forty pound mono for my rig as well, the stiffer line being less inclined to tie itself in knots.

We were in the middle of a December storm, five days when the wind hadn't dropped below thirty knots, the gusts up to fifty. Over the course of the blow I'd managed seven bass over six pounds, two over eight. On the beach I ran into another fisher, the first I'd seen since the weather turned. He was chipper. Seven bass, and he'd kept the best, around fifty centimetres. I watched him fling his gear out. Impressive, it was a pendulum cast and it must have gone eighty-odd yards into the teeth of the blast. 'The last wave,' he said, 'that's the trick.' Now I remember the pendulum from O-Level Physics, but I have no clue how to pendulum cast. I stuck to what I do best, a big juicy razor clam bait and a fifteen yard lob into the margin. Two between six and seven pounds, both released, and one fat fish that went eleven-and-a-quarter and served as a Christmas roast for some friends. The other chap had six more from the deeper water while I was there, the biggest about three pounds.

• When I lived in the US my work colleagues organised a few trips on party-boats. One outing was on a breezy day. We went aboard and waited for the skipper to cast off. He came on the tannoy: it would be choppy in the channel, anyone who didn't fancy big waves could disembark and claim a refund. One of my pals – a fellow with two advanced degrees – jumped up. 'I'll be back, don't let them leave without me.' He beetled up the gangplank, fiddled with something, then scurried onto the boat. 'What was that about?' I asked him. 'Seasickness tablets. Following the directions. They only work if you take them on dry land. See, the bottle says, 'Take two before boarding the ship.''

- Sound advice for domestic peace: never leave lugworms in the kitchen fridge.

Big hooks, big baits, lots of juice

Really rough water means I have to use a wired lead which says my gear isn't going to be seeking out the bass pubs. And generally the surf's well coloured as well, so I like a bait the bass can find in the murk, and find from a distance. To begin with make it something beefy. A crab, a sandeel, or a bunch of worms is lost in a maelstrom of khaki foam like the bubbles on one of those three quid Italian coffees, so I go for enough bulk to load a pair of 4/0 or 6/0 hooks. Nine or ten inches of tasty treats is ideal. It won't cast too well – large baits mean more wind resistance – but it won't need to. Then as well as size, plenty of scent, a load of juicy razor clams or an unwashed squid, dripping with ink and innards. Once in a while I'll use a mackerel head-and-guts, but this seems to work best only when the day-boats are busy between the storms, plenty of mackerel frames being tossed away. And whatever I choose I tie it up with lashings of elastic thread to secure it against the suck of the surf.

Late November, but the water was still close to fifteen degrees, the air about the same. The breeze was onshore between twenty-five and thirty-five knots, and the rain was gentle. The moon was full and I thought I could see fish swirling in the surf-table, so a couple of large razors and a fifteen or twenty yard lob. My first cast came up with a three-pounder. My second produced a four-pounder. Both decent fish, but this looked like a morning for a Leviathan so I switched to a nine inch squid just as the rain started in earnest. Back to the weather, hood up, and I remembered – too late, Murphy's Law yet again – that I was wearing the wrong jacket, the one with holes at the shoulders.

Then a knock, very gentle, like bootlace weed on the line. A pause and a yard of slack. I tightened into what I thought would be a lump of wrack and felt two slow thumps, quickly followed by a run of eighty yards. After twenty-odd minutes, three shorter runs, and a heart-stopping lunge through the last wave I had a twelve pound bass on the shore – and about a pint of rainwater in my trousers.

• I was on a south-facing beach in a gale. The weed was a pain, the rain was steady, but I managed a few bass so I decided to wrap things up. Bending down to grab my bag I felt an almighty thump on my backside, a thump that left me face-down on the shingle.

I was about to offer some Anglo-Saxon advice to whatever eejit thought it amusing to boot my bottom when I saw the culprit: a twenty gallon plastic drum which had blown in across the waves, then whizzed up the shore and knocked me for six. On the side of the drum were the words, 'Oil, fish-frying.' It seemed like an omen for dinner.

Reliable gear, fresh bait

It's never much fun losing a fish. Losing a big fish is miserable. Losing a big fish because of a dull hook or a failed knot, that's self-inflicted agony, so now we're heading to the GP for a fistful of anti-depressants. But it happens. A churned-up sea brings all sorts of junk into the shallows: weed, rocks with weed attached, bunches of mussels, barnacle-coated driftwood, bits of trawl-nets, lobster-pot buoys, and so on. And any one of these chunks of flotsam can muck up your tackle, blunting hooks, tangling or wearing through monofilament. So in big bass conditions it makes sense to be extra vigilant.

At the end of every cast, as well as testing the hook-points, I check for knots in the leader and rough spots on the line. It's a bit tedious to be faffing with your rig when you want it back in the feeding zone, but not as tedious as losing your dream fish in the shallows.

There's another thing that goes on in rough water. Your bait takes a total pounding, like trousers going through the washing machine on the dangerously grubby cycle, the setting for jeans where you left a razor clam in the pocket for a couple of weeks; and a succulent unwashed squid or an oily half-mackerel soon turns into a lump as bland and soggy as a railway buffet sandwich. So don't wait too long before replacing it with a tastier offering. Again it can seem as if you're wasting precious fishing time, but you're not. Appetising baits catch a lot more bass than tired ones. And if you're anything like me you fish much more keenly and attentively when you know there's something fresh and tempting on your hooks.

- Showery, warm, calm, but the bass were obliging. The sea was jumping with jelly-fry, and I was flicking a muddler minnow through the shallows. As the rain eased I saw a bedraggled marmalade cat padding along the sand, so I called him over and gave him a tickle. I took out the last of my paper towel and dried him off as he purred with evident delight. No sooner had I finished than he gave a flick of his tail, trotted down the beach, walked into the water up to his tummy, and caught himself a mouthful of fry. Then he turned and faced me with that catty smile, the one that says, 'Admit it, I'm a genius.'

- People often come up to me on the shore and ask if I'll sell them a bass. I used to find this insulting. After all if I were picking blackberries they wouldn't try to buy them. But I've realised what's going on, and it's kindness not rudeness: my fishing clothes are so grubby and tatty that I look as if I need the money.

9lb 8oz, whole unwashed squid, early May, in an onshore gale. The gusts were over 50mph and I could chuck my bait only 20-odd yards into the weather, but that was plenty far enough. It's rarely too rough for bass, more often too rough for bass fishers.

Squid's a good bait in wild conditions, big enough and juicy enough for the bass to find it.

I caught one of 9lbs 8oz, mid-November, in the middle of the UK's first named storm, Abigail – A Big Gale, I suppose. The wind was onshore at up to 45mph and the surf was very coloured. There were pilchards in the wave, but not a sniff when I used one as bait. A big mess of razor clam was the ticket, plenty of juice and scent.

I like a bait the bass might already be feeding on, but also one they can find in the conditions. Gungy water calls for something juicy: razor, whole squid, or a blood-and-gutsy half mackerel. And in a big wave it makes sense to keep replacing washed out baits with fresh ones.

Large baits don't cast very well, but that's no problem when you're after the big fish. I almost always find them very close to the shore.

Stealth still matters

In rough and well coloured water it's easy to think the fish won't be frightened away too readily. Crashing surf, a hooting wind, sea like soup, how on earth would they notice anything that happens on the shore? And I don't know how they do it, just that they do. Maybe because they're so close in, big bass can be scared away by pretty small disturbances.

One stormy morning just about first light I ran into a dog-walker. His labrador bounded along the water's edge and I saw two swirls ten yards into the wave, either a training session for the seal-pup Olympics or a couple of monster bass making emergency U-turns for the depths. Luckily I'd already had a good fish, so I was intrigued rather than annoyed. But the lesson's clear: even in wild conditions don't scare off your trophy by flashing light on the water or stomping up and down the strand like the North Korean army. If a soft-pawed retriever's enough to drive the whoppers away, a hefty-booted fisher needs to act like a twinkle-toed dancer – and that's the waltz, not the pogo.

Stay on the move

Only anecdotal evidence but I think large bass don't shift around a whole lot, especially in a thumping great wave. They tend to be solitary as well, perhaps because they need to eat everything they find, they can't afford to compete for their food with hungry schoolmates. Or maybe the babies stay away from monsters for fear of being swallowed. Once in a while I watch fish in daylight. When it's rough the big ones pay no heed to Jan and Dean (*Ride the Wild Surf*, Liberty Records, 1964), they simply loaf about alone, letting the swells push them around in the shallows. I also find that chunky fish tend to take quickly or not at all. I reckon swirly water creates lots of eddies, and these wash the food along and concentrate it in a very few spots. So all a predator need do is find an area where there's plenty of flow and plenty of grub, stake her exclusive claim by driving any smaller fish away, then hang about waiting for the next treat to show up.

From a fisher's point of view a ripping hoolie and a whipped-up sea seem to mean that the fish won't come to you, you need to come to the fish. You don't want to settle into position for too long, keep searching. My normal MO's a short cast, a ten minute wait, a shorter cast, another ten minutes, then up-sticks and try a little hike along the shore.

Keep calm and take your time

When you hook a big bass, you know it. The thumps are slow, like the drum in the Peter Gabriel song about South Africa (*Biko*, Charisma Records, 1980). The weight's unyielding; lively and bouncy, but unyielding. Beware, too much adrenalin turns otherwise sensible people into total eejits. I've seen fishers pumping like mad, rods bent double, desperate to land their monster double-quick. This can end in tears. A hefty, frisky bass in the wave-dump is a recipe for disaster, energetic pumping can result in slack line, and a lot of folk have lost giants right at the water's edge. It must be heart-breaking to see your fish, then have her get away; and often it's a lash-up born of impatience to drag her up the sand before the hook-hold slips. Much sounder to trust your hooks, and with sharp 4/0s or 6/0s there shouldn't be much cause for concern. Then take it gently, wind slowly and steadily, let your whopper have her head, fish a loose drag, allow – or even encourage – a few runs. That way when it's time to bring her through that nerve-shredding final wave she's knackered and much more easily managed.

Trying to gaff big bass in the surf is another way to lose a giant. On a sandy shore you only need a gaff if the fish is too lively to beach; and if she's too lively to beach, I don't want to be the poor sap chasing her through the shallows in the dark. A misdirected swipe or a clumsy wader-booted stumble can part the line or yank the hook out. If it was someone else's bass you were gaffing, it can end a beautiful friendship as well. So don't be in a hurry, play the fish further out to sea, then there's no need for a drama – even a tragedy – at the water's edge.

- When I was a youngster I read that a kipper was a good shore-fishing bait. I've never tried using one. First, I wonder how on earth bass would get used to feeding on them. And second, I love kippers and I'm not willing to share.

- An angling magazine described a fisher as having a smile on his face. It made me wonder: where else would he have a smile, his knee-cap?

CHAPTER ELEVEN

A Week in September

The wind is in from Africa, last night I couldn't sleep.

Sunday

A gentle waft of breeze. Unusually for Cornwall it was out of the southeast – our prevailing wind's westerly, Cornish palm trees bow apologetically to the east – and the forecasters said it was bringing air from the Sahara. I sat in the garden to slurp my early morning coffee, and by four-thirty in the morning my legs were clammy from a fifteen minute tromp in waders. (Speaking of which, why do folk spend money on saunas? A brisk hike in fishing kit works up a dripping sweat even when it's nippy.) Anyway there was a decent froth on the water in my little cove, I clipped on a 135 millimetre shallow diver with a translucent white finish. My first couple of casts were almost parallel with the water's edge. On the second, when the lure was twenty-odd feet from my toes, it stopped dead.

Before I could slacken off to unsnag it, I felt a wild thump, and a fish took off along the shore. Reel buzzing I followed it, stumbling over the football-sized boulders like an overwrought ostrich on roller-skates. Then mercifully my bass headed for the deeper, snag-free water where I could play her more comfortably. About four pounds, a single hook-point through the scissor, an easy release.

By first light I'd had two more bass, one about a pound, one hardly longer than the plug. Also a wrasse and a good table-sized pollack, two thick fillets, so that went into the bag. Then with the sun almost over the horizon I started to feel sharp wriggly hits on almost every cast. Out of curiosity as much as anything else I swapped the diver for a 90 millimetre surface lure. That solved the mystery: a baby mackerel nine or ten inches long, breakfast for the cat.

Monday

A fishless day. I volunteer in a couple of charity shops. The dress-code's casual, but it would be discourteous to the customers to show up smelling of squid or coated with blood, sand, and mackerel scales.

One of my jobs is to sort through incoming donations, and I live in hope of a library of rare angling books or a collection of old Hardy's rods and reel – that stuff sells for a packet, and our shops need more revenue. But mostly I find lots of murder mysteries and smart ladies' skirts and jumpers. Men's togs are a rarity. Women seem to become bored with perfectly respectable outfits and buy new ones. Typical male behaviour is to wear everything until it consists of holes held together with stained and faded fabric.

The breeze dropped away though the day, it was almost uncomfortably hot in the sunshine. On the way home from town I stopped by a south-facing beach for a look at the sea – I often do – and it was as flat as a dab. So in the evening I tied a few undersized feathers, number 1 hooks. Nothing elaborate, just glittery tinsel bodies and hair wings, but I thought they looked spot-on for joey mackerel. And I'd much rather peer at my fly-tying vice than at the brainless drivel on the television.

Tuesday

A late start by my decidedly silly standards, I left the house at about five-thirty. On the end of my local pier fifteen minutes later, the tide half and rising. A harbour's a magical place in darkness, arc lights glaring onto the water, masts and rigging clattering like a melodically challenged steel band. I clipped on a pair of my new joey-feathers with a little wedge on the point, and slung out into the darkness. It didn't take long to find the mackerel, I soon had two good eaters for supper, but what I really wanted was some bait-sized tinkers. And as the light came up so did the little ones, a dozen between seven and ten inches long.

At home I gutted the table fish and froze the tiddlers in vacuum bags. My wife and daughter bought me a food saver device and it's brilliant, one of those rare kitchen appliances that do more than gather dust and serve as drying racks for damp tea-towels. I packed my joeys in sixes. That's a wildly extravagant morning's worth of bait, and I often wind up tossing a few into the briny at the end of my outing. But better that way than running out when the whoppers are on the feed. It's happened to me once: two six pounders, two ten pounders, then my squid bag was empty. Just once, but it was a deeply scarring experience, I'm never going up that gum-tree again, desperately peering down the gullet of a bass in the hope of finding a something only half-digested.

- Ask a true fisher how the trip was and you'll always hear, 'Good'; which means, 'There was some water, and I didn't drown in it.'

Wednesday

Back to the charity shop. Very warm indeed, sweating like a pig in a tropical rain forest. By the end of my shift the breeze was stiffening, south with a hint of east again, and as I drove home the surf looked as promising as a commercial for an expensive moisturising cream.

Thursday

Lying in bed I could hear the wind picking up. It wasn't a proper hooter, that makes a whistling noise around the chimney, but encouragingly fresh. By three-thirty I could stand it no longer, the wave was calling like the sizzle of streaky bacon in the pan, I was on the beach by four. The surf was still building, I'd have liked another foot or so on the breakers, but it would have to do for now. In the carpark I mounted one of my wee mackerel on a pair of 4/0s, plenty of elastic thread to keep the points of the hooks exposed. And at the water's edge I gave the surf a gander before tying on a four ounce bomb. Correct choice, I chucked out thirty-odd yards and I could feel the weight settling for a few moments, then wandering along the bottom.

My first cast produced a hard-fighting clump of bladder-wrack. But thick weed doesn't show up often at the start of a blow, so I toddled along the beach for a hundred yards and tried a slightly shorter lob. Almost at once I felt a tentatively jiggly nibble, nothing like the thump of a bass, then a few inches of slack. It was a conger, just big enough to make the leader into a slimy dream-catcher. I took my rod up to the top of the beach to re-rig – the water was clear, I didn't want the Blackpool illuminations anywhere near it – and tie on another bait.

This one did the job, a bass in a hurry: no preliminary tugs, she picked up my gear and headed straight for America. I didn't bother to measure her. She was lightly lip-hooked, I managed to shake her off without even pulling her onto the sand. Somewhere between five and six pounds. Thirty minutes later I beached her twin sister, unless it was the same fish all over again. Then nothing, total radio silence from bass country.

The first glimmer was showing in the eastern sky, the surf had increased and I was wondering about a switch to a wired lead. But I decided to fish one more cast with the bomb, just a fresh bait. This one was a whisker bigger than the rest, so I snipped its nose off – a spot of blood in the water couldn't do any harm. And sure enough my tackle swung around in the wave, then stopped. A dirty great yank, a pause, and a load of slack line. I backed away up the

A nine inch mackerel rigged on two 4/0 hooks. A little nick behind the head puts some juice into the water, an advantage when it's on the soupy side. My ideas about bait selection are simple. First, try to fish something the bass are eating already. Second, big baits are better than small ones. Third, sight baits in a clear sea, scent baits if it's cloudy. And fourth, don't be stingy, take plenty with you, ideally at least two different types. If the mackerel had drawn a blank, I'd have switched to squid or razor.

Most frozen baits – though not mackerel or sandeel – can be half-thawed and refrozen without losing their effectiveness. And most are cheap or free, so you'd be as dotty as a dalmatian to let yourself run out.

beach to tighten, my reel buzzed as the fish headed away into the deeps, the slow wallops of a heavy metal drummer on valium. Twenty long minutes later I had her in the shallows. I paddled in up to my ankles, ready to try for another hands-free release. But the bait was invisible, swallowed deeply, and a thick trail of blood was pouring from her gills. A keeper by default: 11lb 14oz, ten portions for freezing. Of course I checked her stomach while I had the fillet knife in my hand. No surprise, a scad, five joeys, and the frames of two bigger mackerel.

• Fishing takes place in the overlap between optimism and pathological delusion.

Friday

From Thursday lunchtime the wind dropped away, leaving a lip-smackingly bubbly surf. Also gargantuan amounts of weed. Maybe because the weather was coming from an unusual direction, the beaches were laden with more junk than a car-boot sale on a bank holiday. An early evening recce took me to three favourite spots, not one of them accessible for fishing, waist-deep piles of wrack and jetsam blocking the way. So I shoved my fly-fishing gear into the car in readiness for an early morning estuary jaunt.

By four-fifteen I was at the water's edge, flicking a home-tied whitebait fly into the current. I thought I could hear fish splashing as I wandered along the bank. Autumn's when the peal show up (or finnock, herling, whitling – little seatrout have more aliases than a serial con artist). And sure enough my rod sprang to life as a twelve ouncer zipped up and down the pool. Then a better one, close to a pound and a half. And as the dawn began to show weak in the east I felt the unmistakable double thump of a bass, a two pound schoolie.

Fly-fishing's a delight. There's nothing to carry but a rod, a fly-box, and some mono. Waders produce the laborious gait of a constipated duck, but it's a duck on a stroll, not a back-packing expedition. It's easy to release fly-caught fish as well, no deep hook-ups, no fin-stabbed or gill-sliced fingers. And lastly you're watching a fairly small area of water, you see a lot of detail. I spotted two kingfishers, a pod of baby gilthead bream, and a juvenile seal who mucked about with a flattie like a toddler with hideous table manners.

A building wave, St. Michael's Mount in the background. This spot's almost on my way home from town, just a slight detour, and I often pull over to check on conditions. You can see weed on the beach. In a good blow weed's certain to show up – along with plastic waste, commercial fishing gear, flip-flops, and driftwood. But a long beach gives you the opportunity to move, and that often puts your gear into clear water.

The surf's almost big enough to need a wired lead, but that's a last resort as far as I'm concerned. I'd rather have my bait moving about a bit, seeking out the bassy spots on the bottom.

When I took this snap the bay was full of mackerel, the day-boats were catching them non-stop. So were the bigger bass.

Saturday

The wind had swung into the northwest, flattening the wave on the south-facing beaches. So I bit the bullet and drove up north, twenty-five minutes of wasted time. How people manage long daily commutes in their cars is beyond me, I'd be a long thin streak of permanent blazing road rage.

Anyway the surf wasn't enormous, maybe three feet, but there was a lovely fizz to it. So a joey mackerel, a three ounce bomb, and a confident twenty yard lob into the break. Mistakenly confident, like a Cheltenham Festival punter on the rum-and-ports: half a dozen casts, three hikes along the shore, one bite – which turned out to be a gluttonous weever about as big as the joey. That was enough to dim my enthusiasm for mackerel baits, I thawed a packet of razor clams in the shallows. No more weevers, three school bass and a fat flounder which I kept for the pot. I didn't bother weighing it, but it was a sustaining meal for a pair of good trencher-folk. And of course Saturday afternoon saw me pondering weighty matters – like climate change, the three-thirty at Wincanton, and where to fish on Sunday.

- A Cornish grace ('croust' means lunch):

  God bless us as we eat our croust,
  send sunshine down from heaven.
  Let rain and indigestion fall
  on Somerset and Devon.

- A tip: do up your jacket or take it off. Open zip-fasteners are braid magnets.

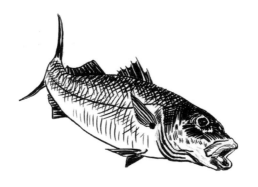

CHAPTER TWELVE

A Future for Bass Fishing

With each step forward there's two looks back

It's easy to be gloomy about the future of our sport. Fifty years ago nipping down to the beach in decent conditions was like going to the butcher's shop. You'd be amazed if the butcher didn't have a piece of beef for Sunday lunch, equally gob-smacked to come back from the shore without a bass for the table. Life in the old days wasn't a complete bed of roses: we ate vast quantities of spam, walked miles to school through the snow, and lived in a small shoebox in the middle of the road. But there was no shortage of bass. In fact they were like mackerel: drop a few off with the neighbours and you'd see their eyes roll as they put on a show of gratitude at the prospect of another cheap fish supper. Ordinary folk preferred cod and haddock, while food-toffs went for Dover sole and imported red

171

mullet. Most of us released a lot of our bass simply because there was nothing else to do with them. And today I meet people – good fishers too – who've hardly ever caught a proper bass in years of trying. Numbers are down, government stock management efforts are the normal public sector triumph of spin over substance, and the marine environment's as full of shite as Glastonbury at the end of the mud and music festival. So a few modest thoughts on how we can turn things around.

None of my ideas is directly or party political. I vote in every election, but my pencil cross seems to be the kiss of death for the candidate I choose; which shows I'm no expert on the workings of Westminster. So I'm not going to recommend marching to the House of Commons and pelting the Honourable Members with rancid ragworms, posting slimy squid to the minister responsible, or hauling trailers up to London and carpeting Downing Street with maggoty seaweed – protests that might be good for a laugh, but not very effective. I write loads of letters to the press, my MP, the Prime Minister, whomever, but I don't expect to make any difference that way. It's just a way to let off steam without subjecting my wife to yet another obscenity-laden rant about the gutless, incompetent, overpaid, integrity-challenged tossers in government.

- Once in a while I run into a fisher who peers at my beach outfit with obvious contempt. 'I only ever fish artificials,' I'll hear, with the sort of tone you'd expect for 'I only ever have sex with bipeds.' Just an opinion, but I think fishing snobs are twits. There's a fine line between being a purist and being a pain-in-the-neck bigot. Live and let fish, I say.

- Find a spot that's an easy walk from a carpark, comfortable underfoot, pleasantly sheltered, not too many underwater snags, you're guaranteed to be in tiddler-central. Obvious really, basic Murphy's Law. So a prediction: the next record bass will come from a mark that can be reached only by hiking five miles through a nettle-strewn bog full of adders then abseiling down a crumbly vertical cliff. The fisher will have to stand on a wrack-coated slimy boulder and cast backwards into an impenetrable kelp forest. And the fishing will be good only when it's thundering, hailing, or both.

So what are some more practical steps we can take to safeguard a future for our sport, to make sure the next generation doesn't see the bass only as a flavourless, plate-sized creature from a fish farm in Cyprus?

Obviously catch limits have a huge part to play and that means more catch-and-release. Reading blogs and articles I see two different opinions about which fish should be going back. Some fishers favour a maximum size limit, where it would be legal to keep smaller fish, but the big breeding females would be returned to the water. On the other hand the regulators and the scientists have come down on the side of minimum limits, ensuring we don't kill bass too small to have spawned. Not being a marine biologist I'm unqualified to offer an informed view on this. I realise that total ignorance doesn't stop self-appointed on-line experts from weighing in with authority on almost any topic, but I'm inclined to listen to the boffins, the people who know what they're talking about. Also common-sense tells me that a maximum limit would be unworkable around the netters who've always caught most of our bass anyway. You can insist on a mesh size big enough to let the tiddlers go, but how would you design a net that avoids whoppers?

One point about catch-and-release where I do have a strong opinion: put fish back quickly. A lot of catch reports end with something about how the bass swam away strongly. Well of course it did unless it was dead already, it wasn't going to hang about in the shallows rubbing its nose on your waders and begging for another lugworm. The real question is whether it survived in the longer term.

And again I'm no ichthyologist but it's pretty clear to me that we do least damage to our fish when we unhook them and have them back in their element with a minimum of out-of-the-water faffing. With a single hook – in a bait, a shad, a fly, or a soft plastic – sometimes you can just run your fingers down the line, give a wiggle, and away goes your bass, untouched by human hand. And there are ways of making almost sure fish aren't hooked too badly. On productive trips I put away my lures with trebles – they're blighters to remove. In the surf I find a held rod and big hooks generally avoid swallowed baits. And even if it takes a bit of unhooking, at least put your bass back right away. (That's why my snapshots are so dull, I never take my camera to the shore. By the time I could work out which fiendishly tiny buttons to push, my catch-and-release fish would be dead, dying, or suicidal from the boredom of waiting for Steven-bloody-Spielberg to find the on-switch. So I only take pictures at home, with bass that already are destined for human digestive systems.)

My next idea's very easy: get more folk bass fishing. Extra rods on the rocks and beaches may put a little bit of pressure on stocks. But more important, tons of pleasure-fishers mean a chance the politicians will take our interests seriously. It's easy to dismiss MPs as a bunch of self-important, unctuous, ignorant, expense-fiddling yahoos, but our elected representatives know they need our votes. And if every car on the road had a rod on the roof-rack, plugs in the glove-box, waders in the boot, and an enticing aroma of stale bait, candidates for office would bend over backwards to work with the bass fishing gang. So how do we boost our numbers? Often I reckon it just takes a spot of advice and encouragement.

I meet plenty of young fishers who've given up on bass – too difficult, too many blanks – and converted to tiddler-snatching (or LRF as they call it these days). Some tell me they can't afford the gear for bass fishing, with flies, lures, or bait. All these folk need is a tip or two to help them see that – in spite of what they may have read in magazines and on websites – you don't have to be a hedge-fund manager or a Russian oligarch to kit yourself up for the rocks or the beach; and you don't have to be a genius or a jammy, lottery-winning son-of-a-gun to land a bass.

> *A summer dawn with lashing rain-showers, I decided to give the surf a miss and see if I could pick up a few mackerel from a local pier. There were three lads fishing already, hoodies, tins of cheap lager, and tiny rods and reels like the ones from seaside shops that sell inflatable toys and hats with tasteless slogans. The young chaps were catching pollack and whiting about the size of my big toe, and they were quite impressed when my Toby produced a few mackerel. I filleted one and free-lined the head about ten yards from the pier. A three pound bass, which I gave them. By the time I headed home my new pals had three bass in their basket – and I reckon they were addicted.*

• Trout and salmon flies have such appealing names: Mallard-and-Claret, Wickham's Fancy, Kite's Imperial, Silver Doctor, Jock Scott, Thunder-and-Lightning. Clouser Minnow, Bucktail Deceiver, and Gummy Sandeel are decent patterns but they sound a bit dull.

Another thing that's easy for any fisher to do is to join something, a nationally affiliated local club, a UK-wide association like BASS, whatever. Groups with lots of members make noises that are heard in the corridors of power. When I write to my MP I'm pretty sure my letters go unread into a folder called 'Peevish-in-Penzance', and the Prime Minister likely files my stuff under 'Crabby-in-Cornwall.' But if the opening line of my bolshy correspondence were to say, 'As chair of the Bass-Maniac Trust I represent 200,000 fishers, 1,100 tackle-dealers, and 250 guides…', they'd pay me a lot more heed. Commercial fishing interests are well organised and well represented in Westminster. Sport-fishers need to play by the same rules.

And that leads to another idea. Let's stop treating professional fishers as the enemy, we need their cooperation. A lot of anglers find it impossible to say the word 'net' without stuffing a bunch of obscenities in front of it. If it's an illegal net, too close to shore or in a bass nursery area, fair enough. But I have no problem with lawful catches – folk have to earn a living after all.

I saw a bumper sticker that read, 'Ban commercial bass fishers.' Luckily it was on a dirty van, so I could use a finger to add my two-pennyworth, 'Starve their children.' Whether we catch bass to have fun or to make a wage, we're all people, mostly decent people. Our interests are the same, to ensure stocks survive. One fine day – along with world peace and an end to discrimination – we'll see fishers of all persuasions working together to manage our shared resource. And that fine day will come a sight quicker if we stop treating the for-profit lot as devils in yellow oilskins.

The folk who set illegal nets are another story altogether, cheats, thieves, and common criminal scum, to put it very politely indeed. In a fairer world these dirt-bags would be prosecuted, their gear would be confiscated – including the boat that set the net, the car that took them to the harbour, the clothes they wore, and their lunch sandwiches – and they'd be left naked and hungry on a motorway hard-shoulder in a blizzard.

In a less satisfying reality all we can do is report unlawful nets to the IFCA. People tell me it's a waste of time calling the IFCA, they don't have enough staff to do anything; and it is indeed depressing how little money's spent on enforcement. So if you provide information about illegal netters, there's a fair chance nothing will happen. But if you don't, it's a racing certainty the reptiles will go unpunished. So it's worth a try at least.

I was on a beach at low water when I found a hundred metre net staked in the inter-tidal area. The mesh was tiny and the catch was finger mullet and baby schoolies. It was hard work, but I dragged the whole ungodly mess to the top of the strand, an access route for earthmovers rebuilding the sea defences. So if you lost your gear, don't blame me, talk to Martin, a huge tattooed fellow in a JCB digger. He's a very keen fisher and conservationist. His friends call him The Crusher, and he'd love to meet you.

• In North America there's a very tasty and popular eating fish that's sold as Chilean Seabass. Until a few years ago it wasn't imported at all and it was called a Patagonian Toothfish. That sounds a good deal less tempting. Maybe we should re-name the bass: 'Inshore Lugworm-Muncher' or 'Mackerel Gut-Swallower' – that would drive down commercial demand.

Another simple step, keep things tidy. It seems the most damaging waste in the oceans is micro-beads, tiny plastic particles too small to see. The chemical companies put them in shampoos and cleansers as little scrubbing agents. In the seas they're eaten by micro-organisms, then they work their way through the food-chain, right up to the top predators. All I can say is that you really don't need hair (I've have none for years), so why not cut down on your use of these toxic little killers?

More seriously there's lots of normal, visible shite on the shore as well. A recent survey found a hundred and sixty water bottles per mile of UK coastline, and that's disgusting. At a minimum fishers can stop dropping their own filthy rubbish, and it doesn't take much sweat to do a bit of a clear-up. You might think the efforts of one or two neat-freaks wouldn't make any difference, but here's something I've noticed: stuff a bag with junk and you can start a chain-reaction as other folk feel the need to do the same. And along with sensible catch limits, cleaner seas should mean more bass.

I walked along the sand, passing three teenagers who'd been fishing all night. Their area of the beach was carpeted with trash – bait-wrappers, cider tins, crisp packets, tangles of mono. If I gave them a talking-to about littering I'm sure they'd have been stroppy.

So I produced a shopping bag. 'Looks like you forgot to bring your rubbish sack, lads. Good thing I've got a spare.' Minutes later one of them came haring towards me across the strand. 'Mister, have you got another of those bags for us? The first one's full, and we keep finding more stuff. Some people are real mucky pups, aren't they?'

11lb 14oz, of which about a pound must have been the joey mackerel and frames in her stomach. I'd planned to release this one, but the hooks were totally swallowed and she was bleeding profusely. Unless the law requires it, I see no point in putting back a fish that isn't going to survive. Why feed the seals, crabs, and seagulls when I can feed myself?

It was unseasonably warm, breezes from the southeast, and I wound up shedding most of my warm togs on the beach. A few times a year I think how great it would be to have breathable waders, but before I get around to ordering them, the weather turns again. And I tend to shred my clothes and boots like a kitten with a favourite jumper, so I'm best served by cheap kit.

- A lot of foodies say you can't trust a thin cook. I'm not sure about that, but I'd never go into a tackle-shop that doesn't smell of squid.

Quotas apart, here's another way to reduce pressure on bass stocks: persuade people to eat other species. Some of the TV chefs have done a good job with pollack, but there are lots of tasty fish that don't show up often on the supermarket counter or the restaurant menu.

Whiting for example, tons around in winter, and they're terrific in strips, deep-fried in breadcrumbs. Dogfish, which most fishers see as a chucker, was a staple when I was a lad. No bones, so nervous parents can feed their kids without fear of choking. The meat has a firm texture, and as long as you skin it promptly it's good in batter or in fish stews and soups. (If it's not skinned in good time it can taste of uric acid; and nobody wants fish, chips, and pees.) Flounder's another species that's overlooked in the kitchen. Catch them from estuaries and they often taste of mud, but from a white sand beach they're every bit as good as plaice in my book. Grey mullet are similar, nasty if they live in harbours, superb from rocks and shingle beaches, with a lovely shrimpy flavour and a delightful chewy consistency. And gilthead and black bream are right at the top of the tastiness tree, but even they don't make it into many fishmongers' shops.

Changing habits around fish-eating could seem like an uphill struggle, but I'm not sure it's as tough as we might think. So much fish is flogged by the big supermarkets that they have a huge influence over what ends up on supper plates. And even though most of us never buy fish – we demand a higher standard of freshness, we wouldn't be caught dead eating other people's catches – we still can steer retailers to offer more varied stuff. We just need to swing by the appropriate counter once in a while and ask after a flounder, a few whiting, a grey mullet, or a portion of dogfish.

A last idea, we're much more likely to be taken seriously by the powers-that-be if we're seen as part of a larger interest group. We're not just fishers, we're also conservationists and users of the great outdoors. Which doesn't mean we all have to join the Green Party, chain ourselves to Japanese whaling ships, or hike the coastal footpath until our eyebrows ache; but it does mean we should see ourselves as representatives of our sport, and we should think about the impression we make on other people on the shore.

That's one reason it's so important not to dump our rubbish. Rusty hooks and tangles of line make us look like environmental hooligans and idle tossers to boot, and that won't win us many friends. Another way of tarnishing our reputation is dealing moronically with unwanted catches.

Once in a while I'll stumble on a pile of dead whiting or doggies on the beach, left to rot by some half-witted so-called sport-fisher. I don't know about you, but I don't want any part of an activity that involves butchering fish then leaving them in a stinking heap, and I imagine these mounds of festering corpses must disgust the dog-walkers and surfers as well. Only once have I run into one of the unmitigated shite-heads who dispose of their by-catch this way. He told me there were too many dogfish in the sea, banging a few on the head was OK. My response: most scientists say the world's overpopulated, so would it be similarly OK if I were to impale him on my sand-spike? I'm not always diplomatic.

But with the folk who come up to me on the rocks or the sand and ask sometimes fatuous questions – like, 'Are you fishing?' – I'm charming. Well, as charming as possible for an old scruffpot in an evil-smelling jacket. Often the first comment I hear is, 'It's so peaceful out here.' I resist the urge to say, 'It was really peaceful until you showed up with your yapping terriers.' Then I chat with them about their dogs, the surfing wave, bass, good local pubs, rip-off parking, and the weather (especially if they're British). Sometimes I nod with studiously feigned fascination as they rhubarb on about football, mobile telephones, or television dramas (of which I know nothing and care a good deal less); because I want them to know that we're all on the same side, we're all human, we all want clean beaches, clean oceans, and a sensibly managed environment for our children and grandchildren. And if we work together, who knows what we can achieve?

The End

MURPHY'S LAW

A few readers have asked about this.

It applies not just to fishing, but to life in general.

The original maxim is, 'Anything that can go wrong will go wrong.'

Alternative versions include:

'Every silver lining is wrapped in a big dark cloud.'

'Whatever you wish for, that's exactly what won't happen.'

'Life will get you in the end, not to mention the beginning and the middle.'

'Blessed are the pessimists because they're always right.'

SONGS QUOTED AT THE START OF CHAPTERS

1 Marvin Gaye *What's going on?*

2 Sam Cooke *A change is gonna come*

3 Bob Dylan *Tombstone blues*

4 Leadbelly *Bring me little water, Sylvie*

5 Hoyt Axton *Lightning Bar blues*

6 Nick Lowe *Rose of England*

7 Neil Young *Ambulance blues*

8 Leonard Cohen *Anthem*

9 Withered Hand *For the maudlin*

10 Ian Tyson *Four strong winds*

11 Joni Mitchell *Carey*

12 King Creosote *Miserable strangers*

Lightning Bar blues is covered by tons of people, but the original is best.
Four strong winds is most familiar by Neil Young, but Ian Tyson wrote it.

Other Fishing Books from Merlin Unwin Books